INSIDE THE FLYING SAUCERS
by George Adamski

What has happened to George Adamski since he wrote the famous incidents in *Flying Saucers Have Landed?* Since the memorable November 20, 1952, when he first made personal contact with a man from another world? Since December 13, 1952 when he was able to make photographs within 100 feet of the same saucer that had brought his original visitor?

Inside The Space Ships is Adamski's own story of what has happened to him since then. It begins with his first meeting, a few months later, with a second man from another world -- his first meeting with one who speaks to him. This second visitor brings him to a Venusian Scout (flying saucer) and this, in turn, brings him to a mother ship. Later lie is conveyed in both a Saturnian Scout and a Saturnian mother ship. Adamski tells us what transpires in these space craft and what the men and women from other worlds have told him.

Adamski's photographs of flying saucers, originally published in *Flying Saucers Have Landed*, have since become world-famous as other witnesses in other parts of the world have succeeded in taking photographs identical with his. Now, however, in *Inside The Space Ships*, Adamski gives us 16 photographs and illustrations, no longer of Scouts (flying saucers) mostly, but of the great space ships from which they are launched. The main group of these photographs was taken in April, 1955, and neither the photographs nor a description of them has ever been published before.

Desmond Leslie, who was co-author with Adamski of *Flying Saucers Have Landed*, provides a foreword to the new book in which he courageously faces the fact that many will be initially skeptical of the astonishing facts now told for the first time by George Adamski.

An introduction provided by Charlotte Blodget, who was Mr. Adam-ski's literary aide in writing his new book, provides a framework which helps to better understand tile book. Mrs. Blodget also contributes a biographical sketch of George Adamski which completes the book.

Adamski's first book, *Flying Saucers Have Landed,* has now sold over 80,000 copies in the United States alone and has been translated into Dutch, Spanish, French and is soon to be translated into most of the other European languages. In spite of the scoffing of skeptics and the bitter and vicious attacks of opponents, a great world audience has collected to read and listen to George Adamski.

http://www.IllumiNetPress.net

--()--

DEDICATION

I Dedicate This Book To A Better World.

I wish to express my deep appreciation to Charlotte Blodget for framing my experiences in the written words of this book.

George Adamski

--()--

CONTENTS

Dedication 2
Contents 3
List of Illustrations 3
Introduction by Charlotte Blodget 4
Foreword by Desmond Leslie 8
Chapter 1 - Return of the Venusian 12
Chapter 2 - Inside a Venusian Scout Ship 16
Chapter 3 - The Venusian Mother Ship 20
Chapter 4 - My First Look at Outer Space 25
Chapter 5 - Meeting with a Master 30
Chapter 6 - Questions and Answers within the Ship 34
Chapter 7 - The Scout from Saturn 40
Illustrations 44
Chapter 8 - The Saturn Mother Ship 62
Chapter 9 - The Laboratory 68
Chapter 10 - Another Master 74
Chapter 11 - Conversation in a Cafe 77
Chapter 12 - Again the Great Master 83
Chapter 13 - Days at Palomar Terraces 91
Chapter 14 - The Banquet and a Farewell 94
Chapter 15 - An Unexpected Postscript 102
George Adamski - Biographical Sketch 105

--()--

LIST OF ILLUSTRATIONS

The Illustrations are located midway through the Text

1. Venusian Scout Hovering
2. Diagram of Venusian Scout Ship
3. Diagram of Venusian Mother Ship
4. Submarine Type Space Ship
5. Mother Ship Releasing Scouts No. 1
6. Mother Ship Releasing Scouts No. 2
7. Mother Ship Releasing Scouts No. 3
8. Mother Ship Releasing Scouts No. 4
9. Diagram of Saturnian Scout
10. Diagram of Saturnian Mother Ship
11. Space Ships Near the Moon
12. Taken from Inside A Venusian Scout
13. Portholes of a Small Mother Ship
14. The Carrier in a Different Light and Range
15. Last Photo of the Venusian Mother Ship
16. George Adamski

--()--

INTRODUCTION

BY

CHARLOTTE BLODGET

In the introduction to this book I wish to begin by stating that while none can help but find the contents deeply fascinating, I am fully aware that incredulity in varying degrees is bound to follow. Some will accept George Adamski's claims that his experiences inside the space slips were real and factual. Many, feeling the sincerity with which he tells his story, will brand him as an honest but self-deluded man and toss his adventures into the category of the mental or psychic. Still others, trained to reject everything not yet proven in the familiar three dimensions, will enjoy writing it all off as a clever hoax.

Although I myself have seen the space ships on several occasions, both here in the Bahamas where I live and at Palomar during the several weeks I stayed there this past summer, I have never been inside one. Nor, to my knowledge, have I ever met a space man. I have, however, met George Adamski. To know him leads to at least one certainty. He is a man of unquestionable integrity.

After reading *Flying Saucers Have Landed,* and since in any case I was headed for California to spend the summer with members of my family, I wrote to Mr. Adamski describing my sightings here and asked if I might call on him. A cordial invitation to do so was the result.

I do not hesitate to state that I made my first visit to Palomar Terraces with heavily crossed fingers. I was quite prepared for anything from a brilliant lunatic to a harmlessly self-deluded man; or perhaps one more California cult conveniently and profitably hung on the horns of the current Saucer interest. What I found was a man far removed from any of these and rather difficult to describe.

My first reaction was that a minor crime had been committed in allowing so inadequate and misleading a photograph to be used on the jacket of his book. (*Flying Saucers Have Landed*) Not only is Adamski a handsome man in a very individual way, but here was a fine face with integrity clearly written on it. It is also, as I discovered during my weeks there, a face from which an expression of kindness and patience never departs. This does not mean that Adamski has evolved beyond the point where the little irritants which raise the blood pressure of lesser beings have entirely ceased to prick him. Far from it! For incidents such as a recalcitrant pipe when functioning as an amateur plumber, or inability to locate a pet hammer, he has a vocabulary as normal as any man's. But his irritation seldom extends to another fellow being. All who find their way to his door, be they bores, pests or bellicose challengers, meet with the same patient courtesy as the intelligent, the charming or the important in a worldly sense. He has, in short, true understanding and compassion. These attributes, coupled with an ever-ready sense of humor, make him entirely approachable in the broadest sense of the word. Nor does he demand that everyone agree with all that he believes or states. His is the true humility which precludes arrogance.

The fact that Adamski possesses more wisdom than formal education is, in his case, an asset, leaving him free of the fetters which too often shackle the academic mind. At the same time, he is amazingly well informed on most subjects, including world events and the causes that lie behind them. Perhaps it is partly owing to this that he is something of a prophet. Apart from an almost total absence of any material acquisitiveness which sometimes leads others to take advantage of him, Adamski emerges as an unusually well balanced man.

I am inclined to believe that the remarkable brand of patience manifested by Adamski must have played a large part in his selection as one of their important emissaries on Earth by our brothers from other planets. Adamski's is not the easy patience content to wait and dream beside a fire or under a shade tree, but patience backed by action. For instance, once he had become convinced of the extra-terrestrial nature of the strange objects he had seen in the skies, he set about getting photographic evidence of their reality. That this was a project of major proportions should be obvious.

Hazards of weather and the length of time involved did not deter Adamski. Actually, five years elapsed (1948 through 1952) before, out of hundreds of attempts, he had one or more successful photographs of each different type of space ship which he had observed. Then only did he consider the initial stage of his Saucer research complete. Since then photographs taken in many parts of the world have been made public, showing *the same type ships* in corroboration of the Adamski photographs.

Leonard G. Cramp, M.S.I.A., made comparative orthographic drawings of Adamski's Venusian Scout and the craft photographed by thirteen-year-old Stephen Darbishire in England (the "Coniston Saucer") and proved the two identical in structure and measurement. These drawings appear in Cramp's book *Space, Gravity and the Flying Saucer* (recommended reading for scientists and the technically minded).*

(*Published in 1954 in the U.S.A by the British Book Centre.)

Before I left Palomar Terraces I suggested that for the benefit of those who inevitably would be asking for "concrete evidence" it might be well to include in this book some kind of witness substantiation on the part of persons who need not remain currently silent because of security or personal considerations; or perhaps photographs of the interior of a space ship, or of some article made on another planet. Although I understood Adam-ski's explanation as to why he felt such evidence would accomplish little, I was still interested in getting reactions to the lack of it from the widely assorted friends and acquaintances whom I would be seeing. These included prominent scientists, journalists, professors of various subjects and sophisticated laymen.

I found a general interest in Saucers keener than I had anticipated. Moreover, not only was there surprisingly little skepticism in regard to the *fact* of these strange craft in our skies, but a readiness to believe them of interplanetary origin. What few could swallow was that George Adamski had seen and talked with our neighbors from other planets and been taken up in their ships.

Lack of any extensive knowledge of outer space was readily admitted. The concept of un-navigable distance between planets is no longer held by many of our scientists, nor does the old yardstick of light-years stand as the basis on which the time element must be computed. The currents of space (for lack of a better term) are admittedly still mysteries to be explored. The conquest of gravity still lies in the future.

Since science has undeniably made gigantic strides within our lifetime, it is sometimes easy to forget that we are as yet infants in our understanding of the vast Universe of which we are so small a part. We overlook the continual pattern throughout the history of mankind that dictates the enforced abandonment or modification of yesterday's suppositions and conclusions in the light of next day's further discoveries. The more mature the mind of man becomes, the more fully he realizes that the endless miracles of an infinite creation cannot be fully measured by any yardstick he will ever devise. This is a thrilling, not a frightening or discouraging realization. Only the immature mind quickly rejects as impossible or alarming all that which lies outside his own small physical experience or beyond the understanding of his limited imagination.

As a student of history and human nature, Adamski is fully aware that in recounting experiences so far removed from ordinary events on this troubled planet he is laying himself wide open to attack from predictable sources. And although I realize that any aspersions which may be cast upon his sanity or veracity have no power to disturb him personally, I also know what importance he attaches to spreading the truth about the space ships and their *friendly* mission to the divided peoples of our Earth. Because of this, and since I did encounter the demands for "concrete evidence" to substantiate Adamski's claims, I wrote to ask again if he could agree that something along that line might be incorporated in this book. I feel that his reply to me justifies his point of view far more tellingly than I or anyone else could set it forth. Therefore, I asked and received his permission to quote from his letter as follows:

Palomar Terraces

Star Route, Valley Center, California

Dear Charlotte:

I have read your letter with a great amount of interest, and while all the different phases seem to make sense on the one hand, on the other they do not. I don't wish to criticize anyone, but most people who have been trained in one particular field, regardless of who they may be or what position they bold, are often dominated by a too faithful adherence to the traditional and conventional grooves.

As I have told you, I do have witnesses to one of my journeys in a space craft. Both are scientists who hold high positions. Once they are able to make a statement the picture will change overnight. However, the way things are nowadays with everything classified as security, for the time being they must remain in the shadow. When they believe that they can release the substantiation they have without jeopardizing either the national defense or themselves, they have said that they will do so through the press. How soon that will be, your guess is as good as mine. But because they were with me at the request of the Brothers, some things are moving in behalf of both the Brothers and the general public that otherwise could not have been started. And much as we would like to, we cannot speak of these things yet because good intentions can have bad reactions. Anything acted upon prematurely can ruin the best beginnings.

Besides, remember that there is also another side to this matter of evidence, of which you are fully informed and understand the reason why we must wait in patience for the fulfillment of our hopes. Just the other day I received a letter indicating that such possibilities are showing and it seems that eventually support will come from that source, which would be a blessing to the world. So again I have to wait with faith, letting time be the judge.

I can see your point about personal witnesses who, free from security or personal reasons, would be at liberty to speak out and support me. But just as skeptics would question my own affidavit, would they not question that of anyone else? This was proven in regard to the sworn testimony of witnesses present at the meeting described in *Flying Saucers Have Landed*. When a critic is a critic, one can bring the Almighty before him and still he will question. Even the average man is quick to doubt anything that is new to him.

When it comes to concrete articles made on another planet which I might produce, would they really serve? Quite apart from the impossibility of showing them to all readers of the book, we are up against the same old story in regard to photographs of such things. Can you not anticipate such comments as "Adamski concocted this or that and photographed it," -- or "What's so different about this goblet, or that piece of material?" And indeed, judging from anything I personally saw aboard the space craft, there is actually no more superficial difference between a Venusian goblet and ours than between the thousand and one widely varying types manufactured here on Earth!

Look what they have said about the space craft photos which show objects *entirely* different from any made on Earth -- and which have been photographed by many people in different parts of the world! So, no matter how you look at it, unless the person himself has that something necessary to recognize truth, it would make no difference what was presented as evidence, he still would want concrete proof *to suit his own understanding,* ignoring all the other minds in the world.

It is almost like this: he who has the depth of life within his being needs none of these, but he who has not, as Jesus said, "shall ask for signs, but no signs shall be given," for if they were, the doubters would not understand them. His words are just as true today.

He who has the truth asks not for proof, for his inner feeling recognizes that truth which is in itself proof. And we have an outstanding corroboration of this in respect to *Flying Saucers Have Landed.* As you know, I am nobody, living by preference in the mountains rather than in a city where I could meet "all the right people." In that book was plenty of material for the psychologists, psychoanalysts and professional critics to work on -- and they did! Yet the book has gone round the world. You read many of the letters we received and saw that, while a few were of a skeptical and critical nature, most of them were praising. You noted how many people told of their own personal experiences of which, because they too could present no "concrete proof," they feared to speak; or, had tried to tell to friends and relatives -- with unhappy results!

Was it not the so-called professed authorities in times gone by, as they are today, who criticized and disparaged everything proposed for the betterment of man? The kind of proof demanded was premature and could not in wisdom be given. But time and patience finally vindicated those who brought forth the ideas. Humanity is that much better off today because of *them* -- *not* because of the skeptics! It is no different today. But let me assure you of one thing. The Brothers will not fail us if we follow their guidance, any more than they failed us in *Flying Saucers Have Landed*. While we humans did very little in spreading it that far, someone else must have assisted greatly. Therefore, let us follow through without too many changes in the procedure which started with the first book. I am sure that we shall not be wrong. Let the critics ask! Their very opposition may serve as a stimulant for their own curiosity, causing them to enter into a deeper research or analysis. The truth will always prevail in spite of personal or limited opinions.

In regard to analysis of the little piece of metal slag to which I refer in the book and which you held in your hand, I have hesitated because of a former experience. Some years ago I bad a chemical analysis made of a piece of metal alloy which I knew for a fact did not stem from this planet. My first thought was an analysis and I turned it over to a scientist to have done. When I first telephoned to ask the result, this man sounded very excited. But when I saw him later in his laboratory, he had drawn himself under control (or someone else had) and tried to brush the whole thing off lightly.

When he said that it was nothing that could not be picked up in any old scrap-yard, naturally I persisted in demanding an explicit statement of his findings. He then admitted that there were "slight differences" in composition from any usual alloy, but said that could have happened by a variation in heating or some "slight accident" which had gone unnoticed at the time, thereby making duplication of the alloy improbable.

That experience taught me a lesson and I have no desire to risk losing the little piece of metal slag you saw, and which I *know* to be "not of this Earth" by turning it over to anyone until I can be certain that the truth is sincerely sought and will be released.

I recognize that my wisdom is very little in comparison to that of the Brothers. Therefore, I leave all decisions to them, as you would. I have reason to believe that they are endeavoring to make contacts in other parts of the world so that no one, even the most skeptical, could accuse me of perhaps deluding a witness companion, or even buying him off to support my statements, should I try to introduce one whose name carried no weight in the world.

Perhaps the Brothers from other planets are waiting until the inner being of men on Earth stirs ever so slightly toward a wakening stage, with desire for a better living amongst his fellowmen. Perhaps faith is of paramount importance; not blind faith, but that knowing faith which comes only from within and cannot be swerved from what it *knows* to be true. The first book did contribute to such an awakening. The purpose of this book is to stimulate this activity into even greater growth and understanding.

No *scientific* support of any kind was present for the events described in the first book. But events that have taken place since publication, and coming from different parts of the world, have proven greater support than anything that I could have produced on publication date. This has happened in spite of opposing forces who, for whatever reasons, do not wish the truth to come out. It will be the same with this book. I have been well protected against many things, as well as guided. So far, the Brothers have never let me down. So if we wait patiently and in quiet confidence, things will come out as they should. There will be more abundant proof throughout the world than I, as one man, could ever be given or, in turn, give out. Always,

GEORGE ADAMSKI

--()--

FOREWORD

BY

DESMOND LESLIE

When I co-authored *Flying Saucers Have Landed* with George Adamski, I had never met him. My publisher and I both agreed that there was sufficient evidence, in his testimony that he had contacted a Flying Saucer on the ground, to warrant publishing his narrative. Later events proved that we were justified. In November 1958, one month after our book had been published, an object almost identical to the one photographed by Adamski flew over Norwich, Norfolk, and was observed by seven members of the British Astronomical Association and the Norwich Astronomical Society, one of whom, Mr. Potter, made a drawing showing a Saucer with a dome and a ring of portholes, almost identical in appearance to Adamski's photographs.

On February 15, 1954, two boys aged thirteen and eight took a photo of an object that had descended from the clouds over Coniston, Lancashire. The photo was somewhat out of focus but sufficiently clear to show the Saucer, the dome, four portholes and a kind of ball landing gear, similar to the Adamski photographs. The only difference, so far as rough examination could show, was a difference in angle. This photograph appeared to have been taken at an angle of about 250 to the vertical axis of the Saucer, whereas the corresponding Adamski photograph was taken at an angle of about 500. A thorough investigation proved that the boys had not (1) faked the negative, or (2) photographed a model copied from the Adamski photographs. Further evidence was later provided by Leonard Cramp, M.S.I.A. (author of a recent scientific book called *Space, Gravity and the Flying Saucer),* who, by a process of orthographic projections, proved that the Coniston Saucer was identically proportioned to the Adamski Saucer, and that had the boys made a model they would have been first required to make orthographic projections and then build up their model to scale. This would also have required the cutting of several true parabolic curves on a lathe. The boys had no access to a lathe, and knew nothing of orthographic projections, and I doubt if they knew how to cut parabolic curves.

Many had accused Adamski of photographing a lamp-shade. The appearance of a large "lampshade" over Norwich and, later, its sudden descent from the Lancashire skies, suggest that the "lampshade" in question must have been possessed of amazing self-propelled qualities, including the ability to fly across the Atlantic, six thousand miles from California. Also, it might as well be noted that, had Adamski photographed a lampshade or any other manufactured object, presumably -- sooner or later -- a second and similar object off the same production line would turn up in someone's possession and be identified. Adamski's negatives were examined by Cecil B. de Mile's top trick-photographer, Fey Marley, who declared that, if they were fakes, they were the best he had ever seen, and also by Joseph Mansour, chief of Jetex Model Aircraft, who said that in his opinion they were not photographs of models but of large objects about thirty feet or so in diameter.

I went to America and examined all Adamski's films and equipment in the summer of 1954. He has a fine six-inch Newtonian reflector telescope. Over the eyepiece he fits a most primitive kind of camera, consisting merely of a box, a bulb-operated shutter and a slide at the back for plates. This camera fits directly over the eyepiece of the telescope which acts as its lens.

Using this equipment I photographed a model Flying Saucer suspended at some distance. The results looked exactly like a model Flying Saucer suspended at some distance.

Witnesses to Adamski's desert contact of November 20, 1952 told me their own stories. They had watched the big, wingless cigar-shaped ship when it came over Desert Center that morning. They had seen Adamski talking to another person who was dressed in a single garment of brownish hue. When they joined Adamski after the visitor's departure, they had all examined the two sets of footprints in the desert -- Adamski's and another set the size of a woman's "size four." Plaster casts were taken, one of which I now have on my desk as I write. Adamski's footprints lead back to the group; the other set simply vanish at the point where the Saucer had been hovering.

I visited the exact location this August and found that even though the air temperature was around 100° F., my feet left well-defined footprints. I attribute the firmness in the sand to the fact that I was standing on an old watercourse and that there was possibly moisture underneath.

All six witnesses to Adamski's contact -- Dr. and Mrs. George Williamson, Mr. and Mrs. Al Bailey, Mrs. Lucy McGinnis and Mrs. Alice Wells -- affirm that low-flying Air Force planes were circling and swooping during the whole episode; this has never been confirmed or denied by the Air Force.

Adamski was not the first to claim contact with a landed space craft. Six months earlier (June 1952) a mechanic named Truman Bethurum, who was engaged on a construction job on the Mormon Mesa, Mojave Desert, claims to have made several contacts with the crew of a large Saucer who invited him aboard. Bethurum struck me as having far too little imagination to have invented his story. It also turned out that his boss, E. E. White of the Wells Cargo (not Fargo!) Construction Company had seen the Saucer come in to land from a distance of one-and-a-half miles and had presumed, in the fading light, that it was a disabled airliner. And on a later occasion White and several others saw two members of the Saucer crew. I do not believe Bethurum fully understood what he had seen nor what had been told him by his strange visitors, but only that he did have some kind of experience with an extra-terrestrial object and its crew. As is so often the case, the story improves with the telling. But there is an original tape-recording in which he, frightened and worried, haltingly tells what had happened to him while it was still fresh in his memory.

My own impressions of Bethurum were that he was a good-natured and unimaginative, simple but sincere man in much the same sort of difficulty as would be a native of the Brazilian jungle trying to describe to his village the helicopter that had landed and of the amazing white-man crew within it.

With Daniel Fry it was a different story. Fry was a government engineer working at White Sands Testing Ground, New Mexico, in 1950. One evening, according to him, a small Saucer landed and a voice invited him aboard (coming from a kind of radio, for the ship was remotely controlled from a mother ship) and explained to him the outline of its construction and propulsion.

Fry's document is the opposite of Bethurum's -- technical, precise -- typical of an engineer used to facts and figures. Fry claims his contact took place four years ago, but at the time he told very few people for be was afraid he would lose his job or be considered mad.

Shortly after I met him he volunteered (some say he was coerced) into undergoing a lie-detector test on TV. Fry, being an engineer, took the precaution of making his own test to see if he could detect lies from the lie-detector. For this he deliberately gave a false age, place of birth, etc., which the detector recorded as truthful answers. Concerning his own experience, the detector recorded untruth. After this, one of our investigators, Mme. Manon Darlaine of Hollywood, wrote concerning this to her friend J. Edgar Hoover, chief of the F.B.I. Hoover replied that the lie-detector was totally unreliable as it merely registered emotional changes, and for that reason he had condemned its use in criminal investigation. Fry's personal tests, made without the knowledge of the operators, fairly well proved that this particular investigation was useless.

All three men, Adamski, Bethurum and Fry, claim that their experiences are concrete and physical, having nothing to do with the psychic realm. They are realistic in their conversation, pointing out that, as far as they can see, they merely happened to be present when members of a more advanced civilization paid us a visit -- nothing more. They struck me as reliable men, anxious to tell the truth, who admitted that it was hard to recall so great an experience in ordinary words. They have all suffered as a result of their experiences. No doubt the natives who reported the jungle helicopter landing suffered a]so from disbelievers and the superstitious alike.

While on the subject of the superstitious, it is worth noting that the lunatic fringe of untrained psychics have moved into Flying Saucers with a grave danger of discrediting the whole business.

It would be sad indeed if the truth should become lost under a smoke screen of self-important nonsense. For if Saucers are real, then our planet stands on the verge of the greatest scientific, sociological and philosophical discoveries since the dawn of time.

An associate from South America, Ed Martins, came up to Mt. Palomar while I was staying with Adamski in July, bringing several landing reports from South America which seemed to follow the same pattern -- large circular ship, good-looking normal human beings within, powerful electromagnetic force-field surrounding the ship. From Canada we received personal reports from a watchmaker named Mr. Galbraith who lives near Swastika, Ontario. In 1948 he claims to have seen two large ships land. On both occasions a man got out and collected some samples of soil from the ground. The man appeared friendly. But the force-field emanating from the ship was so powerful that -- to use Galbraith's words -- "it flattened the grass and set me back on my heels." On the second occasion a police patrol was searching the woods for an escaped criminal. They saw the light in the forest but were unable to approach, encountering, they said, an invisible wall. Galbraith, too, says that this "wall" of energy prevented his approaching, although he could plainly see the ship (he was on the other side of the wood) whilst its occupant smiled at him reassuringly. This invisible "wall" figures in some of the recent reports of landings from France and Italy. The trouble with these European reports is that they were nearly all made by terrified farmers. When a man is frightened he cannot clearly record what he has seen. An associate, Jef Athierens, a reporter in Belgium, told me he had personally interviewed some of these farmers. He was convinced that they had seen "something very unusual land," but what it was is hard to determine owing to the fear element which negates accurate observation.

There have been many other landing reports in the past two years: some have turned out to be obvious hoaxes -- of which category there will undoubtedly be many more to come. I do not believe they are all crackpots and hoaxers. The only trouble is that against their testimony we have the whole weight of modern astronomy which claims to have pretty well proven that life in our form on other planets in this system is impossible. Either one or the other must be wrong. It is all too easy to dismiss a mere handful of men when we have "science" to back us up, but that is the lazy way out. The claims that the world was round, that wax could record sound, that the ether could carry radio waves, that rays could penetrate and "see inside" matter, that a heavier-than-air machine could fly, have all been dismissed in their day as impossible and contrary to scientific knowledge. The latest book to appear concerning the planet Mars has been written by Dr. Hubertus Strughold *(This Green and Red Planet)*. It proves that if our instruments and their information are correct, intelligent organic life as we know it could not last ten seconds on Mars. But Strughold ends by admitting that perhaps we have overlooked "some crucial factor" and really the only way to be quite sure is for us to travel to the other planets for ourselves and find out firsthand.

There is an alternative -- that men from these strange worlds come to visit us first. That they reveal to us a little of their art, their life, their lore, their science, their religion and philosophy from which we may benefit a little.

That is exactly what some people swear by their life has already happened. George Adamski, for one, tells of the many illuminating hours he spent in the company of men from more highly evolved worlds and he has managed to recapture some of the spiritual beauty of their knowledge and philosophy.

At first, there appear to be only two ways in which you can take this amazing document. Either it is true or it is not. I cannot prove to the reader it is true anymore than I can prove it is not. Each will have to decide for himself.

But really it is a little premature for argument. The main thing is to read it and study the teachings given, for they can be of great help and benefit to many. By the time they have been widely absorbed and (one hopes) applied, others who have had similar experiences will come forward to support the claims of this lone pioneer.

The first to launch a new truth (or rather a recurring aspect of the One Truth) upon the world has invariably met with ridicule, scorn arid cries of "Fraud!" The pioneer is by nature a few decades ahead of his time and is abused by his fellowmen, whose grandchildren scratch their heads and wonder what all the fuss was about, because to them the full fruits of the lonely pioneer have become everyday and commonplace fact.

Until then Adamski finds himself in the same awkward position as the native of Brazil who was given a ride in a helicopter. He's had his ride. The helicopter has gone away. He tries to tell his tribe what happened but there are no words in his language to describe it adequately. However, using the simple speech of this Earth Adam-ski has done his best to record an experience that was not of this Earth. To relate such an experience in its totality would be impossible. It must of necessity be colored by the personality and narrative style of the teller, as is a]-ways the case.

But, despite these difficulties, Adamski has managed to give us a glimpse of a civilization we might well envy; a civilization our grandchildren maybe fortunate enough to enjoy. On whom will decision rest? Who shall decide whether future generations shall tread the starry ways and listen to the music of the spheres or whether they, deformed mutations, live in caves and scratch the poisoned soil with primitive picks to eke a wretched living in a world of horror triumphant?

We shall! The decision rests with us. Humanity has presented itself with a final ultimatum -- live the *Life* or perish forever. Into this snake-pit of quarreling atomic giants and muddled frightened people comes a flash of light. It radiates down from a beautiful crystalline ship in which we believe are men who have mastered their passions and would help us master our own -- if we would let them. We cannot afford to ignore them. We are in no position to sit and split hairs when the very foundations of this planet are teetering on disaster.

Read, then, the following with an open mind and see whether the light of its teaching rings true.

--()--

CHAPTER 1

RETURN OF THE VENUSIAN

Los Angeles is a city of lights and noise, of rush and restlessness, in striking contrast to the quiet starlight and peace of my mountain home. It was February 18, 1953. I had not come to the city for excitement, but because I had been drawn there by the kind of urgent impression described in *Flying Saucers Have Landed*.

Following a custom of many years when visiting Los Angeles, I registered in a certain downtown hotel. After the bellboy had brought my suitcase to the room, received his tip and departed, I stood uncertainly in the middle of the floor. It was only about four o'clock in the afternoon and since I literally did not know what had brought me here, I felt rather at a loose end. I went over to the window and stood staring out at the busy street. There certainly was no inspiration there.

Coming to a sudden decision, I went downstairs, crossed the lobby and wandered into the cocktail lounge. The attendant knew me and, although originally skeptical, after talking with me and seeing my photographs of the Saucers, had become keenly interested. He greeted me cordially. After we had chatted a bit he said that a number of people had become interested in his Saucer reports and had asked him to give them a call if I should come in.

He waited for my reaction and I hardly knew what to say. Momentarily at least, I had no plans. While I did not feel particularly like giving an informal lecture to a group of strangers, on the other hand it seemed as good a way as any to pass the time while waiting for . . . well, whatever I *was* waiting for!

I gave my consent and soon quite a gathering of men and women had assembled. Their interest seemed sincere and I answered their questions to the best of my ability.

It was nearly seven o'clock when I excused myself and went a short way down the street to have dinner. I chose to be alone, with only the persistent feeling of "something is going to happen" for company.

After eating in a half-hearted kind of way, I returned to the hotel. There was no one in the lobby whom I knew, and the bar had no further attraction for me.

Suddenly, I remembered Miss M -- , a young lady student of mine who lived in the city. She had been unable to come up to our mountain place for some time and had asked me to call her when next I came down. I went into a telephone booth and dialed her number. She seemed delighted to hear from me. Having no car, however, she explained that it might be an hour or so before she could arrive by streetcar.

I bought an evening paper and, to avoid encountering anyone who might recognize me, *I* took *it* up to my room. After I had read what was of interest to me, I forced myself to wade though items I would ordinarily have skipped; this in an attempt to discipline the restlessness which now permeated my entire consciousness.

Before the hour was up I went down to the lobby to wait for Miss M -- and she arrived about fifteen minutes later. We talked for quite awhile and I succeeded in straightening her out in regard to a number of problems which, locked in her mind, had grown out of all proportion. Her gratitude was touching and she told me that she had constantly been holding the thought and hope that I would come to the city and help her.

As I walked with her to the corner where she took the streetcar, I wondered if the urge that had reached me in the mountains could possibly have been her telepathic message getting through. But when I was quiet again in the hotel lobby I knew this could not be the explanation. That feeling was still with me -- stronger than ever!

I looked at my wrist watch and saw that it said ten-thirty. The lateness of the hour, with still nothing of extraordinary significance having taken place, sent a wave of disappointment through me. And just at this moment of depression, two men approached, one of whom addressed me by name.

Both were complete strangers, but there was no hesitancy in their manner as they came forward, and nothing in their appearance to indicate that they were other than average young businessmen. Because I had lectured in Los Angeles, made appearances on radio and TV, and also been visited by a great many people from that city at my Palomar Gardens home, such an approach from strangers was not an uncommon experience.

I noted that both men were well proportioned. One was slightly over six feet and looked to be in his early thirties. His complexion was ruddy, his eyes dark brown, with the kind of sparkle that suggests great enjoyment of life. His gaze was extraordinarily penetrating. His black hair waved and was cut according to our style. He wore a dark brown business suit but no hat.

The shorter man looked younger and I judged his height to be about five feet, nine inches. He had a round boyish face, a fair complexion and eyes of grayish blue. His hair, also wavy and worn in our style, was sandy in color. He was dressed in a gray suit and was also hatless. He smiled as he addressed me by name.

As I acknowledged the greeting, the speaker extended his hand and when it touched mine a great joy filled me. The signal was the same as had been given by the man I had met on the desert on that memorable November 20, 1952 .*(Described in the book Flying Saucers Have Landed.)*

Consequently, I knew that these men were not in-habitants of Earth. Nevertheless, I felt entirely at ease as we shook hands and the younger man said, "We were to meet you. Have you time to come with us?"

Without a question in my mind, nor the slightest apprehension, I said, "I place myself entirely in your hands."

Together we left the lobby, I walking between them. About a block north of the hotel, they turned into a parking lot where they had a car waiting. They had not spoken during this short time, yet inwardly I knew that these men were true friends. I felt no urge to ask where they proposed to take me, nor did it seem odd that they had volunteered no information.

An attendant brought the car around, and the younger man slid into the driver's seat, motioning me to get in beside him. Our other companion also sat with us on the front seat. The car was a four-door black Pontiac sedan.

The man who had taken the wheel seemed to know exactly where he was going and drove skillfully. I am not familiar with all the new highways leading out of Los Angeles, so I had no idea in which direction we were headed. We rode in silence and I remained entirely content to wait for my companions to identify themselves and explain the reason for our meeting.

I realize that such a trusting attitude ordinarily would seem foolhardy in the light of the lawlessness rampant in our world today. But it was an attitude followed by men of other civilizations in the presence of men recognized to possess greater wisdom than they. This custom has also been practiced by the American Indians to show respect and humility, patience and faith. I understood this well and conducted myself accordingly, since in the presence of these men I sensed a power which made me feel like a child in the company of beings of vast wisdom and compassion.

Lights and dwellings thinned as we left the outskirts of the city. The taller man spoke for the first time as he said, "You have been very patient. We know how much you are wondering who we are and where we are taking you.

I acknowledged that of course I had been wondering, but added that I was entirely content to wait for this information until they chose to give it to me. The speaker smiled and indicated the driver. "He is from the planet you call Mars. I am from the one you call Saturn."

His voice was soft and pleasant and his English perfect. I had noticed that the younger man also spoke softly, although his voice was pitched higher. I found myself wondering how and where they had learned to speak our language so well.

As the thought passed through my mind, it was immediately recognized. The Martian now spoke for the first time since our meeting in the hotel. "We are what you on Earth might call 'Contact men.' We live and work here, because, as you know, it is necessary on Earth to earn money with which to buy clothing, food, and the many things that people must have. We have lived on your planet now for several years. At first we did have a slight accent. But that has been overcome and, as you can see, we are unrecognized as other than Earth men.

"At our work and in our leisure time we mingle with people here on Earth, never betraying the secret that we are inhabitants of other worlds. That would be dangerous, as you well know. We understand you people better than most of you know yourselves and can plainly see the reasons for many of the unhappy conditions that surround you.

"We are aware that you yourself have faced ridicule and criticism because of your persistence in proclaiming the reality of human life on other planets, which your scientists say are incapable of maintaining life. So you can well imagine what would happen to us if we so much as hinted that our *homes* are on other planets! If we stated the simple truth -- that we have come to your Earth to work and to learn, just as some of you go to other nations to live and to study -- we would be labeled insane.

"We are permitted to make brief visits to our home planets. Just as you long for a change of scene or to see old friends, so it is with us. It is necessary, of course, to arrange such absences during official holidays, or even over a week end, so that we will not be missed by our associates here on Earth."

I did not ask whether my companions were married and had families here on our planet, but I had an impression that this was not the case. For a few minutes silence again remained unbroken as I thought over the information they had given me. I found myself wondering why I had been singled out to receive their friendship and been given this knowledge by men from other worlds. Whatever the reason, I felt very humble, and very grateful.

As I was thinking about all this, the Saturnian gently said, "You are neither the first nor the only man on this world with whom we have talked. There are many others living in different parts of the Earth to whom we have come. Some who have dared to speak of their experiences have been persecuted -- a few even unto what you call 'death.' Consequently, many have kept silent. But when the book on which you are now working reaches the public, the story of your first contact out on the desert with our Brother from the planet which you call Venus will encourage others from many countries to write you of their experiences."*(After the book, Flying Saucers Have Landed, was published, the truth of this prediction was proven)*

I felt not only a strong confidence in these new friends, but an overwhelming sense that we were not actually strangers to one another. I also had a deep conviction that these men could answer all questions and solve all problems concerning our world; even to performing feats impossible to Earth men if they deemed such necessary and in keeping with the mission they had come to perform.

We drove on smooth highways for a long time, possibly an hour and a half. I still had no idea in what direction we were traveling, except to sense that we were entering desert country. It was too dark to observe details of the surroundings. My mind continued to be absorbed in reviewing what they had told me and, as I have said before, there was little conversation.

I was jarred out of my musings when, suddenly, we turned off the smooth highway into a rough, narrow, corrugated road. The Martian said, "We have a surprise for you!"

We passed no cars on this road, along which we drove for about fifteen minutes. Then, with mounting excitement, I saw in the distance a soft-white glowing object on the ground. We stopped within about fifty feet of it. I estimated it to be some fifteen to twenty feet in height and I recognized its close resemblance to the Saucer, or Scout, of my first meeting almost three months earlier.

As we came to a stop, I noticed that a man was standing on the ground beside the glowing craft. After we had stepped out of the car my companions called out a greeting. The man by the Scout appeared to be working on something connected with it. The three of us walked toward him and, to my great joy, I recognized my friend of the first contact -- the man from Venus!

He was dressed in the same ski-type flying suit that he had worn on the first occasion, but this suit was light brown in color with orange stripes at top and bottom of the waistband.

His radiant smile made it clear that he shared my happiness over this reunion. After greetings were exchanged, he said, "As we were coming down a small part of this little ship broke, so I have been making a new one while waiting for you to arrive."

I watched curiously as he emptied the contents of a small crucible onto the sand. "The timing was perfect," he said. "I was just completing the installation as you drove up."

It suddenly struck me that he was speaking English with only a slight trace of accent, whereas on our first meeting he seemed unable to speak our language at all. I hoped that he might explain this, but as he did not, I refrained from questioning.

Instead, I stooped and cautiously touched what appeared to be a very small amount of molten metal which he had thrown out. Although still quite warm, it was not too hot to be handled, and I carefully wrapped it in my handkerchief, which I placed safely in an inner pocket of my coat. I still have this bit of metal in my possession.

Although my companions were laughing at my antics, there was no trace of ridicule in their merriment. The Venusian asked, although he must have known the answer, "Why do you want that?"

I explained that I hoped it might furnish proof of the reality of their visit and told him that people usually demanded what they called "concrete evidence" to prove that I was not just "making it all up" when I told of my first meeting with him.

Still smiling, he answered, "Yes, and you *are* a race of souvenir hunters, aren't you! However, you will find that this alloy contains the same metals found on your Earth, since they are much the same on all planets."

Here, I believe, is as good a moment as any to say to my readers that no names, as we know them, were given to me for any of the people I met from other worlds. The reason for this was explained to me but cannot be given here in full. Suffice it to state that there is no involved mystery connected with this but rather an entirely different concept of names as we use them.

While this no-name state created no awkwardness in my actual encounters with these new friends, I realize that it certainly would do so for the reader, especially in the latter part of this book as contacts mount. Therefore, since we of this world are dependent on our own kind of names for one another, I shall provide them.

While I want to make it very clear that the names I am introducing for these new friends are *not* their correct names, I wish to add that I have my own good reasons for choosing them, and that they are not without meaning in relation to those who will bear them throughout these pages.

The Martian I shall call Firkon. The Saturnian is Ramu. My name for the Venusian will be Orthon.

--()--

CHAPTER 2

INSIDE A VENUSIAN SCOUT SHIP

Shortly after our arrival, Orthon turned and entered the ship, motioning for me to join him. Firkon and Ramu immediately followed. As I have stated, the Scout rested solidly on the ground and only a small step up was required to enter the craft.

Although when we had first reached the waiting Scout

I must have anticipated something of this kind, now that I was actually aboard, my joy can only be imagined. As I took a first quick glance around, I wondered if their purpose was merely to show me what one of these Scouts looked like inside, or -- I hardly dared let the hope live -- perhaps actually to take me on a journey though space. ...?

We went directly into the one-room cabin compartment through a door high enough to permit Ramu, the tall Saturnian, to enter without stooping. As he, the last to go in, placed his foot on the cabin floor, the door silently closed. I was aware of a very slight hum that seemed to come equally from beneath the floor and from a heavy coil that appeared to be built into the top of the circular wall. The moment the hum started, this coil began to glow bright red but emitted no heat. I recalled that I bad noticed just such a bright coil on the Scout of my first contact. But on that occasion it had thrown off various colors -- red, blue and green -- like a flashing prism in the Sun.

I scarcely knew where to look first. I marveled anew at the unbelievable way in which they were able to fit parts together so that joinings were imperceptible. Just as I had been unable to find any trace of an entrance door into the Scout of my first encounter, now there was no sign of the door that had closed behind us; only what looked like solid wall.

Everything had seemed to take place simultaneously -- the door closing, the soft hung as of a swarm of bees, the glow of the upper coil and the increase of light within the craft.

It was all so exciting that I was obliged to take myself firmly in hand in order to concentrate on any one thing. I wanted to leave this ship with a clear picture of everything in order to give a lucid account of what I was seeing.

I estimated the inside diameter of the cabin to be approximately eighteen feet. A pillar about two feet thick extended downward from the very top of the dome to the center of the floor. Later I was told that this was the magnetic pole of the ship, by means of which they drew on Nature's forces for propulsion purposes, but they did not explain how this was done.

"The top of the pole," Firkon pointed out, "is normally positive, while the bottom, which you will notice goes down through the floor, is negative. But, when necessary, these poles can be reversed merely by pushing a button."

I noticed that a good six feet of the central floor was occupied by a clear, round lens through which the magnetic pole was centered. On opposite sides of this huge lens, close to the edge, were two small but comfortable benches curved to follow the circumference. I was invited to sit on one of these and Firkon sat beside me to explain what was going on. Ramu took a place on the opposite bench, while Orthon went to the control panels. These were located' against the outer wall between the two benches, directly opposite the now invisible door though which we had entered the Scout.

When we were seated, a small flexible bar fell into place across our middles. This bar was either composed of, or merely covered with, a kind of soft rubberized material.

Its purpose was obvious -- a simple safety device to prevent falling forward or losing balance.

Firkon explained, "Sometimes, when a ship is thoroughly grounded, a sharp jerk is experienced when breaking contact with Earth. Although this does not very often happen, we are always prepared." He smiled and added, "The same principle exactly as the safety belts in your own planes."

It was still difficult to believe that anything so wonderful was actually happening to me. Ever since my first meeting with the Venusian, after he had gone and I was left with an unutterable sense of loss and a longing to go with him, I had hoped and dreamed that one day such a privilege might be mine. Now that it seemed certain we were preparing for a journey into space, I could scarcely contain my joy. Again and again I reminded myself that I must memorize all that I would see and learn, that I might share my experience with others, however inadequately.

"This ship," Firkon continued, "was built for a two-man crew, or three at the most. But in an emergency a great many more can be safely crowded into it. However, this is not often necessary.

He did not explain further and I wondered if by "emergency" he could mean a rescue mission should another Scout find itself in trouble. So impressed was I by this firsthand viewing of the amazing results of their scientific knowledge that it was almost impossible to visualize failure of any description. I had to remind myself that, after all, they too were *human beings* and, no matter how far advanced beyond us, must still be subject to error and vicissitude.

I turned my attention to the graphs and charts that covered the walls for about three feet on either side of the door that I could not see, and which stretched from floor to ceiling. They were fascinating, entirely different from anything I had seen on Earth, and I tried to guess their purposes. There were no needles or dials, but flashes of changing colors and intensities. Some of these were like colored lines moving across the face of a particular chart. Some moved up and down, others crisscross, while still others took the forms of different geometric figures.

The meanings and functions were not explained to me, and I doubt if I could have understood it all, but I noticed that all three of my companions were alert to the changes taking place. I received the impression that the instruments indicated, among other things, direction of travel, the approach of any other object, as well as atmospheric or space conditions.

The wall for a distance of about ten feet directly behind the benches on which we sat appeared to be solid and blank, while on those beyond, opposite our point of entry, were other charts somewhat similar, yet differing in certain ways from those I have described. The pilot's instrument board was unlike anything I could have imagined. The best comparison I can think of is that it looked rather like an organ. But instead of keys and stops there were rows of buttons. Small lights shone directly on these, so placed that each illuminated five buttons at a time. As far as I can remember, there were six rows of these buttons, each row about six feet long.

In front of this board was a pilot's seat, very similar to the benches on which the rest of us were sitting. Close beside this bench, conveniently placed for easy use by the pilot, was a peculiar instrument connected directly to the central magnetic pole.

Firkon corroborated my unspoken guess as to its use by saying, "Yes, that is a periscope, something like those used on your submarines."

As I watched the various lights flashing across the faces of the charts and wall graphs, now increasing, now diminishing in intensity, it became quite clear why these translucent ships are so often reported as changing color as they move through our skies. But there are other contributing factors. Many of the color changes and the glowing coronas which often surround the Saucers are the result of differing intensities of energy radiating out into the atmosphere and making it luminous directly surrounding the ships, due to a process somewhat similar to ionization.

Within the craft there was not a single dark corner. I could not make out where the light was coming from. It seemed to permeate every cavity and corner with a soft pleasing glow. There is no way of describing that light exactly. It was not white, nor was it blue, nor was it exactly any other color that I could name. Instead, it seemed to consist of a mellow blend of all colors, though at times I fancied one or another seemed to predominate.

I was so engrossed in trying to solve this mystery, and at the same time to see and absorb every detail of this amazing little craft that I was quite unaware we had taken off, although I did suddenly register a slight feeling of movement. But there was no sensation of enormous acceleration, nor of changes in pressure and altitude as would be the case in one of our planes going at half the speed.

Nor had we experienced any jerk as we broke contact with the ground. I had an impression of tremendous solidity and smoothness, with little more realization of movement than of the unnoticeable journey of the Earth itself as it revolves around the Sun at eighteen and one-half miles per second. Others who have been privileged to ride in these Saucers also have been struck by the same sensation of movement -- or rather, the almost total lack of it. But the fact is, with so many wonders crowding my consciousness, it was only later, after I was back on Earth reviewing the night's experiences in my own mind, that I could begin to sort them out.

My attention was now called to the big lens at my feet. An amazing sight met my eyes! We appeared to be skimming the rooftops of a small town; I could identify objects as though we were no more than a hundred feet above the ground. It was explained to me that actually we were a good two miles up and still rising, but this optical device had such magnifying power that single persons could be picked out and studied, if so desired, even when the craft was many miles high and out of sight.

"The central pillar or magnetic pole serves a double purpose," explained my bench companion. "Besides providing most of the power for flight, it also serves as a powerful telescope with one end pointing up through the dome to view the sky, and the other pointing down through the floor to inspect the land below. Images are projected through it into the two big lenses in the floor and ceiling, as you can see."

He did not explain whether this was done electronically or by some other means. Its magnifications could be varied at will, and I suspect that there was more to it than a simple optical system such as we know on Earth.

I looked up into the translucent dome. The stars had always looked near enough to touch in the clear air of my mountain home, but viewed through this ceiling lens they seemed to be actually on top of us. As I alternated between watching the wonders of the sky and the swift Earth flashing beneath us, I noticed four cables which appeared to run through the floor lens (or immediately below it), joining the central pole in the form of a cross.

The Martian, noting my change of interest, explained, "Three of those cables carry power from the magnetic pole to the three balls under the ship which, as you have seen, are sometimes used as landing-gear. These balls are hollow and, although they can be lowered for emergency landing and retracted when in flight, their most important purpose is as condensers for the static electricity sent to them from the magnetic pole. This power is present everywhere in the Universe. One of its natural but concentrated manifestations is seen displayed as lightning.

"The fourth cable," he continued, "extends from the pole to the two periscope-like instruments, the one beside the pilot's seat and the other directly behind his seat but close to the edge of the center lens, as you can see. These instruments are really extensions of the main optical system and enable the pilot to see everything that is going on without leaving his seat. They can be switched on and off, or adjusted at will, so that both members of the usual crew can have full use of the telescope without interfering with each other."

All the machinery was beneath the floor of this compartment, and under the outer flange, as clearly shown in the photograph of this Scout.' I did not actually see any of it, but I was shown into a very small room which served both as an entrance to the compartment which contained the machinery, and as a workshop for emergency repairs. Here there was a tiny forge and a few storage cupboards in which, I surmised, necessary tools and materials would be kept.

It was while I was looking through the door into this room that our pilot said, "Be prepared for landing. We are near our mother ship."

I could not believe it. It seemed that only a few minutes had sped by since we had entered the Scout.

Just a moment earlier the wall behind the bench on which we had been sitting had appeared solid. Now a round hole began to appear! I watched in astonishment while it continued to open, rather like the iris of a camera. Shortly, a porthole about eighteen inches wide appeared. This, then, explained the portholes in my Saucer photographs, of which till now I had seen no sign. (The photograph referred to is numbered 1 in the list of illustrations in this book. -- Editor)

Like the door by which we had entered, their coverings fitted so closely as to be undetectable when closed. Recalling what my photos had shown, I reasoned that there must be four portholes on each side, making a total of eight.

"That is correct," Orthon nodded in corroboration, "and the touch of a button can open them all or singly -- and of course they are closed in the same manner."

As the pilot alerted us to our impending landing, the Martian said, "You will be interested to watch this!"

At the prospect of actually landing on a mother ship, my emotion rose to a point impossible to describe. Fighting for composure, my mind framed the question as to where the mother ship was waiting, and in what manner we would make the landing.

Instantly Orthon answered both unspoken questions. "This is the same large mother ship that alerted you and your party on the desert last year at our first meeting. She has been waiting for us up here and is at the moment about forty thousand feet above your Earth. Watch and you will see how these small ships land and enter into their carriers."

Fascinated, I peered out through the portholes. There, below, I was able to make out a gigantic black shadow motionless beneath us. As we came nearer, its huge bulk seemed to stretch away almost out of sight, and I could see its vast sides curving outward and downward. Slowly, very slowly, we drew nearer until we were almost on top of the great carrier. I was not astonished when my companion told me that she was about one hundred and fifty feet in diameter and close to two thousand feet in length.

The spectacle of that gigantic cigar-shaped carrier ship hanging there motionless in the stratosphere will never dim in my memory.

--()--

CHAPTER 3

THE VENUSIAN MOTHER SHIP

Our little craft glided down toward the top of the mother ship, very much like an aircraft coming in to land on the deck of an aircraft carrier. As I watched, a curved hatch or opening appeared, reminding me of a great gaping whale. Those who have seen the photographs of this ship will recall that it has a blunt nose sloping slightly downward. This hatch was situated at the far end of the main cylindrical body just before the slope of the nose became perceptible. As we touched down, the Scout moved forward into the hatch, tilting downward as it began its journey into the interior of this mighty ship. Here for the first time I had a feeling of dropping in the pit of my stomach. I imagine this was due to the fact that the Saucer was no longer using its own power but was now subject to the gravity of the mother ship.

We traveled on down at not too steep an angle, the flange of the Scout running on two rails slowly and smoothly, its rate of descent controlled by friction and the magnetism in the flange. Orthon had complete control over this, I found, for once I nearly lost my balance and he stopped the craft momentarily while I regained it. Then the slow, smooth glide continued until we had reached what I judged to be the halfway position between the top and the bottom of the mother ship. Here the Scout stopped, and the door instantly slid open.

I saw a man standing outside on a platform about fifteen feet long and six feet wide. He was holding something that looked like a metal clamp attached to a cable. He was not very tall -- I should guess about five feet, five inches -- and I noticed that he was of a darker complexion than any of the space people I had seen. He was dressed in a brown flying suit similar in color and style to the one worn by Orthon at our first meeting. Black hair showed from under a dark, beret-type cap.

I followed Firkon out of the Scout and Ramu came after me. Orthon was the last to leave. The man in the beret smiled and nodded to each of us as we stepped off the platform, but no words were exchanged.

From this platform a flight of about a dozen steps led down to one of the decks of the huge craft. As I was guided down them, I had time to notice that our Scout had stopped just before reaching a junction in the rails down which we had come. One pair of rails continued through the ship, curving downward out of sight. Between them was a dark space which prevented any view of what lay below. The other pair of rails continued straight on from the junction before which the craft was halted, and ran astern to a huge hangar or storage deck in which I could see several identical Scout ships lined up on the rails.

"This is the storage hangar in which the small craft are carried during interplanetary flight," explained Firkon, stopping momentarily on the step beside me. "Had we been going on to another planet, our Scout would have stopped at the platform only long enough to let us out. Then it would have passed over the junction and been switched to its place in this large hangar. But because we shall be returning to Earth later, the Scout must be recharged at this platform."

I glanced back and saw that the man on the platform had already slipped the clamp attached to the cable over the flange of the Scout so that it contacted both the flange and the rail beneath.

I have no idea how this recharging operation was performed; to me the clamp looked much like a machinist's large clamp used on Earth. Nor could I see to what the other end of the cable was connected. Perhaps contact between clamp and rail was necessary to complete the circuit or for all I know, it may even have fitted into an unseen connection directly below the rim of the Scout. I did not wish to cause further delay by asking.

Although not answering the question in my mind, Firkon did volunteer, "These smaller craft are incapable of generating their own power to any great extent and make only relatively short trips from their carriers before returning for recharge. They are used for a kind of shuttle service between the large ships and any point of contact or observation, and are always dependent on full recharging from the power plant of the mother ship."

At the bottom of the steps we entered a large control room, rectangular in shape but with rounded corners. This room, I should say, was about thirty-five by forty-five feet, and something like forty feet in height. Except for two door openings, the walls were entirely covered with colored graphs and charts like those in the Scout, but on a larger scale and more numerous.

Extending along all four sides of the room were three tiers of platforms from which the many instruments could be observed and studied. A master telescope stood on the top platform, and another on the bottom platform. From both of these were electronic extensions to many instruments in other parts of the ship, making it possible, I was told, for these two telescopes to be used from many locations on the ship.

Also in this room was a robot instrument which I was cautioned not to describe. I had noticed a miniature version of this robot in the Scout. There were also several pieces of machinery in this control room, none of which, so far as I could see, had any moving parts.

I would have liked to stop in this room for closer observation of all these graphs, charts, colors, machinery and instruments, and to have been permitted to ask questions concerning their operation, but this privilege was not granted. Instead, we went directly through this control room and through a second door which led into the most beautiful living room or lounge that I have ever seen. Its simplicity and splendor took my breath and I gasped as I stood momentarily in the doorway, not only marveling at the richness of its furnishings, but held m the wonderful emanation of harmony that came from it.

I do not know how long it took me to recover from this unexpected experience but eventually I was able to look about me with more interest for detail.

The ceiling, I judged, was about fifteen feet high, and the room could not have been less than forty feet square. A soft, mysterious blue-white light filled it, and yet I saw no lighting fixtures, and nowhere any inequality in brightness.

Then, as I stepped through the doorway into this luxurious lounge, my attention instantly was absorbed by two incredibly lovely young women who arose from one of the divans and came toward us as we entered.

This was indeed a tremendous surprise as, for some reason I had never visualized women as space travelers. Their very presence and extraordinary beauty, the friendliness that was so apparent as they approached to greet us, together with the luxurious background in the out-of-this- world craft, were overwhelming.

The shorter of the two women touched my hand in the recognized greeting, then immediately turned away to walk over to another part of the room. Then the taller and seemingly younger girl leaned forward and touched my cheek lightly with her lips. The first lovely lady returned holding a small glass of colorless liquid which she held out to me.

Stirred deeply by the warm friendliness of these people, I thanked her and took the glass. The water (for that is what it proved to be) tasted like our own pure spring water. It seemed, however, a little denser, with a consistency something like a very thin oil. As I sipped it, I strove to regain my composure and to impress the images of these gracious and beautiful young women indelibly on my mind.

The one who had brought me the water was about five feet, three inches in height. Her skin was very fair and her golden hair hung in waves to just below her shoulders in a beautiful symmetry. Her eyes, too, were more golden than any other color and held an expression that was both gentle and merry. I had the feeling that she was reading my every thought. Her almost transparent skin was without blemish of any kind, exquisitely delicate, though firm and possessed of a warm radiance. Her features were finely chiseled; the ears small, the white teeth beautifully even. She looked very young. I judged that she could not be much over twenty years of age. Her hands were slender, with long, tapering fingers. I noticed that neither she nor her companion wore make-up of any kind on their faces or fingernails. The lips of both were a natural deep red. They wore no jewelry of any description. Indeed, such adornment would have served only to detract from their own natural beauty.

Both women wore draped garments of a veil-like material which fell to their ankles, and both robes were bound at the waist by a striking girdle of contrasting color, into which jewels seemed actually to be woven.

The garment of the little blonde was of a pure light blue, and her tiny sandals were golden in color. Later, I learned that she was a citizen of the planet we know as Venus. Kalna is the name I shall give her.

Ilmuth, my name for the other woman, was taller and a rich brunette in coloring. She also wore her hair in a cascade that fell to just below her shoulders, and it was a beautiful wavy black with highlights of reddish brown. Her large eyes were black, luminous, with flashes of brown. They held the same merry expression as those of her companion, and I felt that she, too, could read my innermost thoughts. In fact, this is an impression I have received from every person that I have met from worlds beyond our own. The color of this lovely brunette's robe was a pale, rich green, and her sandals of a copper hue. Ilmuth, like Firkon, was an inhabitant of the planet Mars.

I realize that in trying to describe these ladies from other worlds than ours I am attempting the impossible. Perhaps, using my inadequate description as a stepping stone, the reader will search his own imagination for an image of perfect beauty -- and then know that it must certainly fall short of the reality.

As I finished drinking from the small goblet of water, I was asked to be seated, an invitation I gladly accepted.

On the wall exactly opposite the door through which we had entered hung a portrait which I was certain must represent Deity. The emotion which the beauty of the two young women had aroused in me was momentarily forgotten as the wonderful radiance emanating from the portrait enveloped me. It showed the head and shoulders of a Being who could have been eighteen to twenty-five years of age, in whose face was embodied the perfect blended balance of male and female, and whose eyes held a wisdom and compassion beyond description. I do not know how long I was enrapt by this beauty. There was no interruption until I myself returned to an awareness of my surroundings.

I did not need to ask who this Being was. Kalna broke the silence by saying, "That is our symbol of Ageless Life.

You will find it in every one of our ships as well as in our homes. It is because we keep this symbol always before us that you will find no age amongst our people."

On one side of the room was a long table surrounded by many chairs. I had the impression that this table was used by the ship's company for meals, and perhaps also as a council table. I had an idea that the number of crew members ran into three figures, although I had seen only a few on this occasion. I received no verification of this latter impression, but my feeling about the table was substantiated by Firkon. I also learned that the greater part of the room was used as a lounge by the crew and their guests when crew members were not at their various posts during flight. The rest of the salon was casually strewn with divans, settees and chairs of different designs and sizes, very much in the manner of Earth. But in every case these were lower and more comfortable than ours, and more graceful in design and appearance. They were covered in a material of a deep soft nap with a brocade effect. The colors varied and were most attractive to look at -- rich, warm and subdued.

Beside the chairs were low glass or crystal-topped tables with interesting decorative centerpieces. But I saw nothing the least like an ash tray. I suppose I knew instinctively that these people were not addicted to the nicotine habit and I left my cigarettes in my pocket. Once, however, through sheer force of habit, I reached for them. Observing this, the little lady from Venus smiled and said, "*You* may smoke if you like. I will get you a receptacle for your ashes. You see, only Earth people indulge in that odd habit!"

I thanked her and returned the package to my pocket without taking a cigarette.

To continue with my description -- the whole floor was covered by a single luxurious rug which reached to the walls. Medium brown and perfectly plain, with a deep, soft nap, it was delightful to walk upon.

When we were asked to sit down, I found myself on one of the longer divans between Firkon and Ramu. Directly opposite, at a comfortable conversational distance, was another divan of the same shape and size. Here the two ladies seated themselves with Orthon between them. I still held the empty water glass in my hand, and now set it down on the low table in front of us.

The material of this goblet interested me. It was crystal-clear, without etching of any kind. It did not feel like our glass, nor like plastic. I had no idea of what material it was made, but I received the definite impression that it was unbreakable.

After noting the most outstanding features of the furnishings, I let my eyes roam around the walls. To my right, I noticed a large and beautiful door, slightly ajar, with no knob or lock that I could see. Kalna told me that this led into a storage room, adding, "Our ship often is long absent from our home planet as we travel and study space. Nor do we always stop on other planets during such trips. Consequently, large storage facilities are needed for supplies and equipment.

"The door you see over there in the opposite wall, like the one serving the supply room, leads into a kitchen."

This door gave onto the portion of the room I supposed was used for dining purposes. I was not taken into either of these rooms.

I studied with interest a large picture near the door on the wall to my right. It showed a city which at first glance seemed little different from those on our Earth, except that it was laid out in circular form instead of the series of hard rectangles usual with us. But the architecture was very different. I hardly know how to describe it, for not one of our many architectural styles approximates it in any way. Here was perfection of the graceful lightness and delicacy for which many of our better modern architects are striving but have never quite achieved. It was the kind of city of which men dream, but never see on our Earth. I had guessed, before I was told, that the city depicted here was on Venus, this ship's home planet.

On the other side of the door was yet another painting, a pastoral scene of bills and mountains with a stream running through the farmland. This might have passed even more easily for an earthly scene except that the farmhouses were not scattered around the countryside, but also followed a circular plan. I was told that this arrangement had been found more practical in enabling these farm groups to become small, self-sufficient communities, containing everything necessary to supply all essential commodities for the country folk. On Venus there is true equality in all respects, including allocation of commodities. Trips to the cities, then, need be undertaken only for pleasure or for personal reasons.

On the opposite wall, behind the long table, I noticed a picture of a large mother ship, and I wondered whether it represented the one we were in. But as this thought passed through my mind, the little lady from Venus corrected it by saying, "No, our ship is really very small in comparison. That one is more like a traveling city than a ship, since its length is several miles, while ours is only two thousand feet."

I realize that my readers are likely to consider such dimensions incredible, and I readily admit that I myself was unprepared for anything so fantastic. However, it is necessary to remember that, once we have learned to harness the great natural energies instead of depending on mechanical force, it should be no more difficult to build cities within the walls of gigantic ships than on the ground. London and Los Angeles are cities nearly forty miles wide which were built largely by crude machines and manpower -- a prodigious achievement in itself. Once gravity is mastered, cities in the air for us, too, can become a reality.

"Many such ships have been built," Kalna explained, "not only on Venus but also on Mars and Saturn and many other planets. However, they are not intended for the exclusive use of any particular planet, but for the purpose of contributing to the education and pleasure of all citizens in the whole brotherhood of the Universe. People naturally are great explorers.

Therefore, travel in our worlds is not the privilege of the few, but of all. Every three months a fourth of the inhabitants of our planets embark on these gigantic ships and set out for a cruise through space, stopping at other planets just as your cruise liners stop at foreign ports. In this way our people learn about the mighty Universe and are enabled to see, firsthand, a little more of the 'many mansions' in the Father's house to which your Bible refers.

"In the temples of wisdom on our planets we have many mechanical devices by means of which our citizens also can study conditions in other worlds and systems, and space itself. But with us as with you, nothing can quite take the place of actual experience. So we have built fleets of gigantic ships like the one you see pictured there, which might also be described literally as small artificial planets. They contain everything necessary for the welfare and pleasure of thousands of people over a three-month period. Apart from size, the main difference is that planets are spherical in shape, are divinely made, and move in elliptical orbits around a central Sun, while these little man-made planets are cylindrical and can move through space at will."

An ever-increasing concept of our star-studded heavens unfolded before my mind's eye as I contemplated the information just given me. I wondered to what "other planets" Kalna referred.

Replying to my mental question, Orthon volunteered, "Our ships have not only visited all other planets in our system, but those in systems close to ours. However, there still are planets without number in the infinite systems within the Universe which we have not yet reached."

Here again a wondering thought slipped in as I mentally questioned what they had found on the "other planets" they had visited.

The Venusian's eyes sparkled and a tiny smile flitted across his mouth as he caught my thought. He continued without interruption. "With the sole exception of inhabitants on Earth, we have found the peoples of other worlds to be very friendly. They, too, have gigantic space cruisers for the pleasure and education of their fellowmen. As we visit their planets and are welcomed, they also visit ours as friends. It is to the Earth alone that these passenger cruisers never approach. Nor will they be permitted to do so until your people have a greater understanding of fellowship as well as of the Universe beyond the limiting confines of your own little planet.

"During flights of this kind, those on the cruise have much leisure time, as well as definite hours devoted to learning. When they land on other planets mutually interesting social gatherings are held. In short," and he made this very clear, "peoples of other worlds are not strangers to one another, but all are friends and are welcomed wherever they go.

"We consider planets throughout the Universe as being in one vast sea of life. The far distant planets by the billions which we have not yet visited will be explored when we have further improved our space ships. There are some planets so far out from any in our system that it would take us two or three years to reach them. Whereas, within our system, the distance between planets can be covered within a few hours to a few days."

Reviewing our concept of distance, I exclaimed, "That is staggering to me! How fast do you travel that you can cover such vast distances in so short a time?"

"Speed to us," was the reply, "does not mean what it does to you. For once a ship is launched into outer space, the speed of the ship is equal to the activity in space! Instead of being artificially propelled, as are your planes, ours travel *on the currents of space.*"

I derived some small hope for our eventual progress on Earth when they freely admitted that, in the earliest attempts to conquer space, the inhabitants of Venus and those of other worlds had been faced with exactly the same problems as those that are holding us back today. Once again they stressed that gravity must be overcome as a first principle on the way to space travel.

--()--

CHAPTER 4

MY FIRST LOOK AT OUTER SPACE

At this point, a man who appeared to be about my age entered from a door in the left corner of the room, smiling in a friendly way. Although I had noticed a ladder in that corner which I presumed must lead to an upper deck of the ship, I had seen no door until be entered through it.

Upon his appearance the two girls excused themselves and left through the doorway leading into the control room. Shortly, Ilmuth, the Martian, returned. She had changed from her lovely gown to a pilot's suit of the same style as that worn by the men. The color was light tan with bands of darker brown at top and bottom of the waist belt. I was delighted when she asked if I would like to accompany her to the pilot's compartment.

Firkon joined us and as we three climbed the ladder to the next deck, I noticed Orthon leave through the control room where we had first entered after landing on the mother ship. The elder man and Ramu, the Saturnian, remained in the lounge.

As we walked along the upper deck corridor, Firkon said, "Each of these large ships carries many pilots, who work in shifts of four, two men and two women. Kalna and Ilmuth are pilots on this Venusian ship."

The corridor, like all parts of the craft I had seen, was pleasantly lighted from some invisible source, and led upward and forward into a small room at the end of the large ship.

As we entered this room, a young man who was bent over a chart of some sort looked up, nodded and smiled, but no introductions were made. I presumed he must be Ilmuth's pilot companion.

"This seems a good moment," said Firkon, "to explain a little more about this ship. It is a carrier for twelve Scouts such as the one in which we arrived. Actually, the interior is not nearly as large as one would guess from its outward size. This is due to much of our mechanical devices being installed between walls."

"This particular ship," Ilmuth added, "has four walls or skins. Some have more and some less, depending on their size and the purpose for which they are built."

As I looked at the number of strange instruments within this room, I was curious to know what "mechanical devices" lay between the walls. Firkon said, "I will explain as fully as possible in the few moments available. The entire section of the ship through which we first entered is given over to storage space for the Scouts, except for a large machine shop in which any necessary repairs can be made. In spite of the great skill and care that go into the original construction, parts do break and materials do wear. Much is required of any craft that travels space.

"The pressurizing equipment which maintains a comfortable temperature throughout the ship is installed between the walls, and much else which would require more time to explain than we have just now. Entrance doors leading into the various walls in all parts of the ship make access easy. Each craft carries several mechanics who, working in shifts, are on constant duty to inspect and check all parts.

Therefore, it is seldom that any defect remains undiscovered to the point of giving real trouble."

In this pilot room I could look up or out or down, in whatever direction I turned my head. As Firkon finished speaking, the young man reached out and touched a button. Immediately, further openings like portholes began to appear in what I had thought was solid wall. Then both pilots took their places in small seats on opposite sides of the room. I felt a slight movement and the ship seemed to nose upward.

My heart beat violently as I wondered if perhaps they planned to take me to their planet. The hope was short-lived. It seemed but a moment before the ship stopped and again hovered. Ilmuth smiled up at me and said, "We are now about fifty thousand miles from your Earth." Firkon motioned me to come to one of the portholes as he said, "Perhaps you would like to see what space really looks like."

I soon forgot my disappointment as I looked out. I was amazed to see that the background of space is totally dark. Yet there were manifestations taking place all around us, as though billions upon billions of fireflies were flickering everywhere, moving in all directions, as fireflies do. However, these were of many colors, a gigantic celestial fireworks display that was beautiful to the point of being awesome.

As I exclaimed at this vast splendor, Firkon suggested that I now look back to Earth and see what our own little globe looks like from that distance out.

I did. And to my surprise, our planet was giving off a white light, very similar to that from the Moon, only not so pure as moonlight in a clear night on Earth. The white glow surrounding the Earth's body was hazy, and its size was comparable to the Sun as we watch this body rise above the horizon in the early morning. There were no identifying markings whatsoever to be seen on our planet. It looked merely like a large ball of light beneath us. From here, one could never have guessed that it was swarming with myriad forms of life.

At the fifty thousand mile altitude, the pilots had set their robot control and Ilmuth joined us, explaining to me, "Each pilot room has a robot. These, working singly or together, can fully govern the course of the ship, as well as warn us of any approaching danger."

The male pilot remained at his post and Ilmuth remarked, in explanation, "One pilot in each control room must always be on duty."

She then asked if I would like to have a closer look at the pilot's instruments.

At one side of each seat there was a small instrument which looked something like a tube set in the floor and standing high enough so that the pilot could easily look into it. "This," Ilmuth explained, "is connected with the telescope you probably noticed in the large control or chart room through which you first entered the ship."

At this moment, however, the telescope was not in operation, and I gathered that it was used only when the ship was in actual interplanetary flight, or perhaps also while hovering for observation and study purposes.

The entire floor in this section of the room was composed of magnifying glass like that in the floor of the Scout. But the angle of the ship at this particular moment was such that I would have had to kneel to look through it.

Space and its activity held me transfixed as I strained my eyes in an attempt to see everything that was going on out there. Apart from the firefly effects, I saw a good many large luminous objects passing through space. The larger bodies, so far as I could tell, were not burning, but merely glowing. One in particular seemed to give out three distinct colors -- red, purple and blue. I asked if it could be another space ship.

"No," Ilmuth said with a smile, but did not explain further.

Also I noticed that now and then dark objects of various sizes, darker than space itself, would pass. But none of these moving objects seemed to touch the ship. At times, even the dark objects would become partially luminous. These, I was told, were what we call meteorites, which become visible to us on Earth only as they create friction in passing through our atmosphere.

I asked what prevented them from striking the ship when seemingly they were headed straight for it.

"The ship itself," Firkon explained, "is utilizing the power of nature -- 'electromagnetic,' I think you call it -- and has excess power at all times. Some of this excess is dissipated through its skin out into space for a certain distance, sometimes only a short way, although at times its influence can extend for several miles outward. This acts as a shield against any particles, or 'space debris,' as you on Earth term it, repelling such things by this constantly radiating force."

He went on to explain that all bodies in space are negative to space and are actually moving in a sea of electromagnetic force. Therefore, a negative radiation repels all negative bodies while at the same time it prevents the ship from heating through friction.

I could have stayed for hours enjoying this beautiful sight, but only a short time was allotted before the pilots resumed their seats and we returned to the forty thousand-foot altitude where the ship had been hovering when first we arrived.

There was no perceptible dip nor turn in the ship's motion. The craft's movement was so gentle as to be scarcely noticeable, and the only audible sound was something as slight as an electric fan in operation.

None of us had been provided with special headgear or any device for breathing or balance, but my mind was clearly alert in every way at all times.

I was struck by the fact that all the instruments I had so far seen throughout the ship appeared to be operated by push-buttons. And nowhere did I see anything that even faintly resembled a weapon of destruction. But, after watching the repelling force of nature in space as controlled by radiations from the ship, I had a strong feeling that this force could very effectively be used for self-protection, should such a need ever arise.

Firkon answered this thought by saying, *"Yes,* that is so. As yet, the need has not arisen. Moreover, if the issue Is merely our lives as against the lives of our brothers -- even those belligerent ones of your Earth -- we would allow ourselves to be destroyed rather than to slay a fellow being."

The implications of this simple statement affected me deeply. I could not help but reflect sorrowfully on the so different viewpoint of my fellow men on Earth; of the divided peoples, the nations even now engaged in a race to produce more dreadful weapons of destruction which would bring death, affliction and sickness to ever-increasing millions of their fellow beings throughout the world. I thought of the credo of hatred for "the enemy instilled in the minds of young men as a necessary part of preparing them for killing. For it is not inherent in natural man who understands even a little of his place in Creation to want to kill. I thought of the indescribable blasphemy of prayers addressed to the loving Eternal Father of all, asking Him to bless them in thus betraying the very humanity of their heritage.

Both Ilmuth and Firkon were silent while these thoughts went through my mind. Although I had many times before reflected on just these things, they had never penetrated my consciousness with such poignancy, and I knew that it would remain with me always.

In a moment, Firkon called my attention to an instrument no larger than an ordinary cabinet radio, with a screen similar to a TV set. "With this," he explained, we can picture and register anything taking place on the Earth, or on any planet over which we either pass or hover. Not only do we hear the spoken words, but pictures are picked up and shown on the screen. An internal mechanism breaks these down into sound vibrations, which are simultaneously translated into words of our own language, all of which are recorded in a manner similar to your own tape-recordings."

To further clear this for me, he explained that all words are made up of vibrations or scales similar to a musical octave, just as all melodies are composed of certain notes. By knowing this law one can learn a heretofore unknown language in a short time. When strange vibrations become apparent, these are transposed into picture form, showing exactly what the strange words or their vibrations mean. Needless to say, the tape he showed me was different from any I had ever seen on Earth.

It all sounded to me like a jigsaw puzzle, and my mystification no doubt showed plainly on my face. In any case, Ilmuth laughed merrily and asked, "Would you be surprised to learn that races of people who lived on your Earth many centuries ago thoroughly understood and used the universal laws of sound and vibration?"

I stated that I had long suspected the truth of this.

"Although this knowledge is utterly lost to your present-day civilizations," Ilmuth continued, "a few individuals here and there are awakening to a slight conception of its possibilities. On other planets, these laws are a fundamental teaching in the educational systems. With these as a basis, pupils are able to learn very rapidly in all fields of knowledge and expression."

At this point, Firkon said, "Now we must return to the lounge," and as I stepped back to let Ilmuth precede me, I asked why it was that practically no movement was felt inside this large craft when she had risen from the forty thousand-foot level to fifty thousand miles.

"Quite simply because the ship is built to take care of all that," Firkon answered, and added, "as is done with your own submarines."

Again I was amazed to find how much these people knew about us and our developments on Earth.

"Your submarines," he went on, "move under the surface of the water at great depths, yet the crew feel relatively little of the movement registered by their instruments. And the men are quite comfortable, too, for your ships have been carefully planned. Actually, there is not so much difference between a ship that goes under water and one that travels through outer space, except that our ships are propelled by *natural* power, while yours are dependent on artificial forms of power."

It seemed to me that the difference he mentioned was quite a tremendous one, but I did not say so, and Firkon continued. "When you learn how to use the natural source of power that is everywhere in the Universe, you too will be able to build submarines which, like some of our craft, can rise to the ocean's surface and continue on up through the atmosphere out into space."

This reminded me of two incidents reported early in 1951. In the first, two "missiles" dropped out of a perfectly clear sky into the waters of Inchon Bay, off the western coast of Korea. The missiles fell close to an anchored seaplane tender, the *Gardiner's Bay,* and caused columns of water to rise to an estimated height of one hundred feet. Later, the report said, the "missiles" were seen to rise again from the water and soar on up until lost to sight. The second incident happened off the coast of Scotland and was almost identical with the first.

Firkon, obviously getting my thought, said, "You were quite correct in naming the photograph you were able to take of this kind of ship 'the submarine type.'"

At this point we entered the large salon in which we had left Ramu sitting with the older man. They were still there and speaking in their own tongue. As we approached, they rose, walked toward a small table around which were a number of chairs and motioned us to join them.

These chairs were rather like dining room or office chairs, but proved far more comfortable. As we seated ourselves, Kalna and Orthon joined our group.

On the table were crystal goblets filled with a clear liquid which I found very refreshing. The flavor was delicately sweet with an elusiveness that was tantalizing. The consistency was slightly heavy, of a type to be sipped. I was told the name of the fruit from which this juice was extracted, but could think of no comparable earthly flavor.

The entire time that had elapsed since leaving the Earth to this moment probably was not much more than an hour. But in that little space of time my whole life and understanding had opened to a far greater concept of the Universe than I had gained during the sixty-one years of my total life on Earth.

Now, as we sat around the table, all eyes turned to the older space man as he began to speak. Although it was only later that his stature on all planets was explained to me, it was impossible not to realize that I was in the presence of a greatly evolved being, and the attitude of all present clearly indicated that they, as well as I, felt very humble before him. I learned that his age, in his present body, was close to one thousand years.

The following hour or so, during which he talked to us, seemed as a minute. All listened with complete attention and without interruption to this man of great wisdom.

--()--

CHAPTER 5

MEETING WITH A MASTER

"My son," said the great teacher, "you have been brought here and shown what lies within our smaller craft and this large carrier. You have traveled in each for a short distance only, but far enough to give you much knowledge to pass on to your fellow men on planet Earth. You have seen what outer space is like and that it is indeed constantly active, filled with moving particles from out of which all forms are finally brought into being. There is neither a beginning nor an ending.

"In the vastness of space there are innumerable bodies which you on Earth call planets. These vary in size, as do all forms, but they are very much like your own world and ours, and most of them are peopled and governed by forms like yourselves and like us. While some are just reaching a point where they are capable of supporting such forms as ours, others have not yet reached that stage of development in their growth.

For you must understand that worlds are but *forms,* and they too go through the long period of growth which all forms experience, from the smallest to the largest.

"Each planet moves in co-ordination with a number of other planets around a central Sun, in perfect timing, forming a unit or what you would call a system. In each case, so far as we have learned from our travels, there are twelve planets in a system. Beyond that, twelve such systems are united around a central core comparable to our Sun. These make up what some of your scientists call an 'island universe.' We have reason to believe that twelve such island universes comprise a vast unit in the Father's house of many mansions . . . and so on, without end.

"On our planet, and on other planets within our system, the form which you call 'man' has grown and advanced intellectually and socially through various stages of development to a point which is inconceivable to the people of your Earth. This development has been accomplished only by adhering to what you would term the laws of Nature. In our worlds it is known as growth through following the laws of the All Supreme Intelligence which governs all time and space.

"As you have seen, we travel space as easily as you cross a room. The traversing of space is not difficult to those who have mastered the laws within which all bodies live and move -- planets and men alike. It is then understood that distance between two such bodies in space, or that between worlds, is no distance at all as you conceive of distance in your world.

"Remember, at one time the distance between the '~ bodies of land on your Earth, which you call continents, was considered great, and much time was required to travel from one to another. Now your aircraft have shortened this distance to a relative fraction of the time required in days past. Yet the distances are the same. And so it will be as you extend your knowledge and learn the laws operating in infinite space.

"Another aspect of which as yet you have no conception is that the body of any human being can be as comfortable on one planet as on another. While there are some differences in atmospheric conditions, depending y upon the size and age of the planet, these are little greater than those which you experience on your Earth 1 between sea level and on a mountain several thousand feet high. Certain people are affected by such changes, more than others, but all can become acclimated in time.

Recalling the popular conception of ponderous headgear plus tubes and gadgets, as depicted all the way from the "comics" to serious theories of supposed experts, I wondered if our world was the lowest in development throughout the Universe.

Reading my thought and continuing without interruption, this great teacher said, "No, my son, your world is not the lowest in development in the Universe. Yours is the least developed of those in our own system, but out beyond there are some worlds whose peoples have not yet grown to your standard, either socially or scientifically. Also, there are worlds where development has gone far in the field of science and remained low in the field of personal and social understanding, even though space has been conquered.

"In our system, the peoples of all planets except your Earth are traveling space freely; some for short distances only, while others achieve great distances that take them to systems beyond our own.

"Your understanding of life and the Universe is very limited. As a result, you have many false concepts about other worlds and the composition of the Universe; and so little knowledge of yourselves! But it also is true that there is a growing desire on the part of many on Earth who seek sincerely for greater understanding. We who have traveled the path you now are treading are willing to help and to give of our knowledge to all who will accept it.

"The first fact your people must realize is that the inhabitants of other worlds are not fundamentally different from Earth men. The purpose of life on other worlds is basically the same as yours. Inherent in all mankind, however deeply buried it may be, is the yearning to rise to something higher. Your school system on Earth is, in a sense, patterned after the universal progress of life. For in your schools you progress from grade to grade and from school to school, toward a higher and fuller education. In the same way, man progresses from planet to planet, and from system to system toward an ever higher understanding and evolvement in universal growth and service."

As he gave this illustration, I understood him to mean that individuals on Earth would, when ready, advance to a planet of higher development. I wondered if, one day while still living on this Earth, we would learn the laws that govern space and be able to visit these other worlds as they now could.

The master gave no specific answer to my mental question, but continued, "You on Earth are bound by what you call 'time.' But even according to your estimations of time, when you achieve space travel you will be astonished at the swiftness with which you can reach other planets.

"For this adventure you will have to find new words. You speak of our craft -- you call them Saucers -- as flying, a term which applies to the operation of your own planes. But we do not 'fly' as you mean it. We nullify the atmosphere by a mechanical procedure. You express it as 'suspending gravity.' In this way we are not hindered by atmospheric interference or resistance. This is why our craft are able to make the sharp changes in direction of travel and to move at the speeds that have so mystified your airmen and your scientists.

"We could tell you much about the control of gravity, knowledge that is necessary both for safe leaving or approaching any planet. We would gladly give you this knowledge which has served us so well, except that you have not yet learned to live with one another in peace and brotherhood, for the welfare of all men alike, as we have on other worlds. If we revealed this power to you or to any Earth man and it became public knowledge, some of your people would quickly build ships for space traveling, mount guns upon them and go on a shooting spree in an attempt to conquer and take possession of other worlds.

"You know that there are certain groups in your world who have already made claim for property rights and possession of your Moon for the purpose of using it as a military base. Many Earth scientists are hoping that, in the not too distant future, they will succeed in building space ships like ours for interplanetary travel. It is entirely possible that this will be done. But Earth men will not be allowed to come in numbers or to remain, until they have learned to embrace the all-inclusive life as lived by people of other worlds, rather than the selfish personal life as found on Earth today. And there will be much for you to learn about outer space, for it is on space itself that you will move.

I recalled a simile I had often used, comparing space to a vast ocean in constant motion. And I thought now that, as our ocean liners move on or through the waves of the ocean, so these interplanetary ships move on the waves of the activity in space.

"Yes," the master said, "it is very much like that, and as your scientists work on this principle, more understanding will come to them. For Nature herself will reveal her secrets to all who seek with an open mind.

"As you have been told, we travel space in order to learn. Within our ships are many instruments, some of which you have seen, and many others which you have not yet seen. Although on your Earth you have thrown all our craft into the category of Saucers, we have many kinds, many sizes, for many purposes. The largest have never come within the atmosphere of your world. In fact, they have never come within millions of miles of Earth. We cannot risk the lives of the thousands of people traveling in these gigantic ships, for if anything should happen to force a landing on Earth before your people have grown to greater understanding, ours would be in peril.

"My son, our main purpose in coming to you at this time is to warn you of the grave danger which threatens men of Earth today. Knowing more than any amongst you can yet realize, we feel it our duty to enlighten you if we can. Your people may accept the knowledge we hope to give them through you and through others, or they can turn deaf ears and destroy themselves. The choice is with the Earth's inhabitants. We cannot dictate.

"In your first meeting with our Brother here, he indicated to you that the exploding of bombs on Earth was of interest to us. This is why. Even though the power and radiation from the test explosions have not yet gone out beyond your Earth's sphere of influence, these radiations are endangering the life of men on Earth. A decomposition will set in that, in time, will fill your atmosphere with the deadly elements which your scientists and your military men have confined into what you term 'bombs.'

"The radiations released from those bombs are now going out only so far, since they are lighter than your own atmosphere and heavier than space itself. If, however, mankind on Earth should release such power against one another in full warfare, a large part of Earth's population could be annihilated, your soil rendered sterile, your waters poisoned and barren to life for many years to come. It is possible that the body of your planet itself could be mutilated to an extent that would destroy her balance in our galaxy.

"These would be the effects directly concerning your world. For us, traveling through space could be made difficult and dangerous for a long time to come, since the energies released in such multiple explosions would then penetrate through your atmosphere into outer space.

I wondered whether, and to what extent, if war should actually come to us, they would feel justified in stopping us.

The master answered my mental question by saying, "As you know, with our knowledge of the use and control over energies far more powerful than any our brothers on Earth have as yet learned to use, we could, if we wished, nullify your force with our greater force. But remember what you have been told. We do not kill our fellow man, even in self-defense. We are trying, and shall continue to try, to prevent such a war by bringing to Earth men the knowledge of what they would be doing. For no man wages war except in ignorance."

A light came into his face and his eyes seemed to be looking at some inward vision of beauty as he continued softly, "And no man lives who has never once dreamed of what you call Utopia, or the nearly perfect world. There is nothing which man has ever imagined which is not somewhere a reality. And, therefore, nothing that is not possible of achievement. For you too, on Earth, this is possible. For us on the other planets of our galaxy, it is so now. There are those on your Earth who have exclaimed, 'But how monotonous perfection must be!' It is not so, my son, for there are degrees of perfection just as there are degrees of all things. In our worlds, we are happy, but we do not stagnate. Just as when one reaches the top of a hill seen from below, a further hill comes into view, so it is always with progress. The valley that lies between must be crossed before the next height can be scaled.

"Understanding of the universal laws both uplifts and restricts. As it is now with us, so it could be on your Earth. Lifted up by your knowledge, this same understanding would make it impossible for you to move in violence against your brothers. You would know that the same conviction, inherent in every individual being, which makes him feel that be has the divine privilege of directing his own life and shaping his own destiny, even though it be by the path of trial and error, applies equally to any group, nation or race of mankind.

"Just as there are many downward paths, leading away from progress, so there are many that lead upward. Though one man may choose one and a second man another, this need not divide them as brothers. Indeed, one may learn much from the other, if he will. For in the vastness of the infinite creation, there is no one way that is the only way.

"On your Earth we have heard many times the phrase 'the road to happiness.' It is a good phrase, for progress is happiness and lies all along the upward pathway from its beginning. And happiness makes men brothers in tolerance toward another man's efforts, even though of a different nature from their own.

"There is nothing wrong with your Earth, nor with its people, except that in their lack of understanding they are young children in the universal life of the One Supreme Being. You have been told that in our worlds we *live* the Creator's laws, while as yet on Earth you only talk of them. If you would *live* by the precepts of even what you now know, the peoples of Earth would not go out to slaughter one another. They would work within themselves, their own groups, their own nations, to achieve good and happiness in that section of your world wherein they were born and therefore call 'home.'

"I think the peoples of Earth would be amazed to find how swiftly a change could come throughout the planet. Now that you have the medium for world-wide broadcasting, messages urging love and tolerance for all, instead of suspicion and censure, would find receptive hearts. For the great part of the Earth's population is weary of strife and its aftermath of woe. We know that, as never before, they hunger for knowledge of a way of life that will deliver them. We know that there is fear and confusion in their minds because they have seen and felt the results of two great wars that have served only to foster the seeds of another.

"So, with receptive minds and hearts everywhere on your planet, it is not too late. But there is urgency, my son! So go forth with the blessing of the Infinite Father on your mission, and add your voice to those of others who also carry this message of hope."

--()--

CHAPTER 6

QUESTIONS AND ANSWERS WITHIN THE SHIP

After a moment of silence during which no one stirred, the master rose, and all present with him. He stood for an instant his hands resting on the back of his chair, and looked deeply into my eyes. I shall never forget the expression of great kindness and compassion in his gaze. It was like a benediction, and at the same time I felt a new Strength rise within me.

With a gesture of farewell which embraced all present, he turned then and left the room. The silence remained unbroken for several moments after his departure.

I still could find no words. It was Kalna who broke the stillness by saying softly, "For us, too, it is always a privilege to listen to this great being speak."

Ramu, the Saturnian, deliberately, I am sure, broke the tension. "Now, before we return you to Earth, an interval has been allowed for you to ask questions that may be in your mind. These need not be confined to the serious subject on which the master has just spoken," he added with a smile, "since nothing that interests you will seem trivial to us."

I looked at him gratefully as we all resumed our seats. It seemed to me that Ramu had meant that I could put my questions orally now, in what was likely to be a general conversation, and not rely on mental telepathy. I voiced the one uppermost in my mind.

"Could the drastic changes in our atmospheric conditions, in many places since the bomb tests, have anything to do with the release of that energy?"

"They have, indeed!" Ramu replied, "and we are not guessing. Our instruments have registered those results. We KNOW!"

"I wonder," I said slowly, "if you would care to comment a little further on the reason why, even though war on our Earth would endanger the traveling through space of millions who live on other planets, you still feel *it* wrong to hurt the few in order to benefit the many.

"We will try to explain," Orthon answered. "To all of us who have from birth been instilled with a vision of the whole, *it* is unthinkable to disobey what we know to be the universal laws. These laws are made by no man. They were in the beginning, and will endure throughout eternity. Under these laws each individual, each group of mankind, all intelligent life on each world, must decide its own destiny without interference from another. Counsel, yes. Instruction, yes. But interference to the point of destruction, never."

His questioning look seemed to ask if he had made the principle clearer.

Firkon, the Martian, spoke for the first time. "You understand the power of thought forms. Apart from our physical missions on Earth, all of us must hold firmly to the belief that the peoples of your Earth will themselves awaken to the disaster toward which they are moving."

"I see," I said slowly, as the issue did indeed clarify itself in my mind.

"We know that the power of this thought continually sent out to all our Earth brothers has changed the hearts of many," Ramu stated.

"We also are aware," Ilmuth pointed out, "as are you and many other people on your Earth, that your air forces and your governments *know* that our ships seen in your skies are coming from outer space, and that they can be made and piloted only by intelligent beings from other planets. Men high in the governments of your world have been contacted by us. Some are good men and do not want war. But even the good men on your Earth cannot entirely free themselves from the fear which has been fostered by man himself on your planet throughout the centuries."

"The same is true of your fliers everywhere on Earth," Kalna said quietly, "many have seen our ships again and again. But they have been muzzled and warned, and few dare speak out."

"It is the same with your scientists," Firkon added.

Again I marveled at their knowledge of our world and its peoples. "Then it would seem," I said, "that the answer lies largely with the ordinary man in the street, multiplied by his millions the world over."

"They would be your strength," Firkon quickly agreed, "and if they would speak against war in sufficient numbers everywhere, some leaders in different parts of your world would listen gladly."

I felt that this conversation had contributed much to my understanding and I was filled with hope. Almost without realizing that I was going to do so, I changed the subject by saying, "I wonder if you would explain a little further to me about the mechanism I saw in the pilot's room -- the one that registers sounds that are translated into pictures on the screen.

"Of course," Orthon said. "One of its most important uses is to enable us to learn readily any language. Naturally, those of us who actually live and work on your Earth for a while speak with better accents. Although, with us, as with you, some have a greater aptitude for languages than others and learn to speak flawlessly without any direct contact with the people." Here he smiled and reminded me of the pantomimic conversation carried on at the time of our first meeting, adding, "It was of the utmost importance that I test your ability to send out and to receive telepathic messages. As an outcome of that, you are here now!

"We know well the skepticism of the Earth people in all directions outside of the narrow ruts of personal experience. It was for this reason that the messages I gave you were of a universal character. We knew that, although the understanding of such writings was buried with civilizations that were lost long ago, there are a few people scattered about your present world who would be able to translate them. With such translations, only the determinedly incredulous can still refuse to believe."

"It is fortunate," Kalna said, with her merry smile, "that at least mental telepathy has been accepted as an established fact by the scientists of your world!"

"You know," Orthon said, "we had you under observation for some years before I finally contacted you, and we felt sure that your knowledge of telepathy would be adequate. This was proven in the final test at our first meeting."

"Did you test me in other ways as well?" I asked.

"Indeed we did! You see, inasmuch as you had been photographing our craft for several years, your thoughts were inevitably coming our way. We felt the sincerity of your interest. It remained to be seen if and how you would translate this interest into action, how well you could stand up under the ridicule and skepticism bound to come your way, and whether you would be tempted to use your contacts with us for self-aggrandizement or commercialism."

"You have passed all the tests with flying colors," Ilmuth said warmly. "In the face of all the derision, disbelief -- even when the validity of your photographs was challenged -- we saw how staunch you remained to that which, within yourself, you knew to be true."

This encouragement filled me with happiness and I knew that, with such friends, any faltering would be impossible.

"There was another thing, too, which we had to know," said Ramu, "in regard to your discretion and judgment. For example, there were certain things which the master revealed to you tonight which, as he made clear, must not yet be told to your people. In a world like yours, it is a great temptation for most men to make themselves important by indulging in attention-getting statements. Moreover, the whole of what is now permissible for you to tell cannot, with wisdom, be told to all. This is where your good judgment enters. After all, you have devoted the better part of your life to teaching universal law insofar as you knew it. In doing so, you learned well that it is not only useless, but often dangerous, to give more knowledge than can be absorbed or understood. We know that you will apply this principle to the information you receive from us."

"In regard to telepathy," I said, voicing a question which had been in my mind, "although I am able to use it, I cannot claim really to understand its operation. Could you explain it a little?"

They glanced from one to another, and then laughed. I realized that all present could answer my question and that they had been amused at the courtesy which had prompted each to give the other the opportunity. In fact, as I look back on the entire discussion, I realize how different it was throughout from what happens in our world when two or more people are gathered together. Where we jump in, talk at cross-purposes and constantly interrupt the speaker (who should at least be permitted to come to an occasional full stop), these men and women had, in all cases, spoken without interruption from the others. And none had held the floor by sheer force of verbosity.

As if by common consent it was Orthon who answered. "In your world you have what you call radio, and there are many amateur radio operators whom you call 'hams.' These have certain channels on which they are allowed to operate. These channels, which you refer to as 'ether waves,' enable a person in one location to send a message to a person at another instrument in some far distant place. The two can hear one another as clearly as if they were in the same room. At one time such communication would have been considered fantastic by people of the type of mind which now derides an interplanetary origin for our ships. To this kind of mentality, little that has not already been proven to the point of being sold over a counter is conceivable.

"Thoughts are received and transmitted in exactly the same way as by radio, along certain wave lengths, but minus any instrument. We work directly from brain to brain, and here again distance is no barrier.

However, an open and receptive mind is needed for success. Through all the years that you have been sending thoughts to us, we have answered. This has established a solid cable-like connection between us by maintaining *the* thought waves in a single channel. Whenever your mind is open, we can send you the information you require, exactly as you could receive a message over a telephone.

"You were chosen to meet with me in the presence of witnesses to confirm your experience. We wanted the truth of this meeting to reach as far as possible. And we commend the staff of one of your nation's newspapers is that the mental contacts we have been discussing are which proved brave enough to publish the first account.

"But one thing which we want you to make clear to all is that mental contacts we have been discussing are definitely *not* what your people call 'psychic' or 'spiritualistic,' but direct messages from one mind to another. Explanation of what you call 'psychic' will be given you at another time.

"We call this mental telepathy a *unified state of consciousness* between two points, the sender and the receiver, and it is the method of communication most commonly used on our planets, especially on planet Venus.

Messages can be conveyed between individuals on our planet, from our planet to our space craft wherever they may be, and from planet to planet. As I said before -- and let me make this firm in your memory -- space or 'distance,' as you call *it,* is no barrier whatsoever."

While Orthon was talking, Ilmuth had unobtrusively gone out of the room. Now she returned with a tray on which were goblets holding what proved to be the same refreshing drink I have described before. After she had V distributed the glasses, I said, "About these people from other planets who are living amongst us … has that been going on for long?"

It was Kalna who answered, "Since time immemorial!

Or at least," she corrected herself, "for the past two thousand years. After the crucifixion of Jesus, who was sent to be incarnated on your world to help your people, as had others before him, we decided to carry on our mission in a way less perilous to those concerned than actual birth on your planet. This was made possible by the great advance in our space traveling ships. We were able to bring volunteers in their physical bodies. These men are carefully trained for their mission and receive instructions in regard to their personal safety. Their identity is never revealed except, rarely, to one or another individual for a definite purpose, as with you.

"They mingle with their Earthly brothers to learn their languages and their ways. Then they return to their home planets where they pass on to us what knowledge they have gathered of your world. We have a history of Earth and the happenings thereon dating back seventy-eight million years. Similar histories which were made by men on Earth have been lost with the civilizations that destroyed themselves -- the same pattern of destruction that threatens you today.

"The thing you call 'war' has not existed anywhere else in our system for millions of years. Of course, all planets and their people must pass through the orderly stages of evolvement from lower to higher. But yours has not been an orderly or natural progress; rather, an endless repetition of growth and destruction, growth and destruction.

"There have been Earth men who have left your planet with our help, in order that they might learn from us and, in time, return to their Earthly home and pass their knowledge on to you. But under the conditions existing on your planet today, it is no longer possible to do this, since none could be returned. They could not explain where they had been without being branded as lunatics and confined in a mental institution. Nor, in your present world of multiple identification papers, would the sudden return of someone who had mysteriously disappeared long before be unchallenged by the authorities.

We cannot subject fellow beings to a persecution beyond their endurance. This may give you an even clearer understanding of how, in so many ways, we find ourselves blocked by those we so long to help."

All the natural gaiety of Kalna's expression had been obliterated by one of sadness as she told me these things. Now, as she took her goblet from the low table and sipped from it, she smiled. As she set the glass back, she said, "It is a great pity that we must talk of such sorrowful things -- and still sadder that such woe exists anywhere in the Universe. In ourselves, we of other planets are not sad people. We are very gay. We laugh a great deal."

I found myself deeply moved by this little apology. They were gay people on their planets. Yet they were willing to share the sadness of our Earth, and to strive ceaselessly through the centuries to bring us light.

"We still have one hope left," Ilmuth said, as though trying to cheer me. "We can still come amongst you, and now and again we can make the kind of contact as with you. While your airmen make our landings difficult at present, we are hoping that, when more and more of your people have seen our ships, become accustomed to them and accepted the truth of living beings on other planets, personal meetings with Earth people can be increased."

"I cannot see how it could be otherwise," I agreed.

We all drank from our glasses. As I looked at my friends, I saw that all signs of the concern they felt about conditions on planet Earth had been banished from their faces. I knew that this was wise and right and, trying to follow their example, I asked, "Do you dance and sing on other planets, and have parties as we do?"

"We dance a great deal -- all of us," Kalna answered. "We consider training the body in a coordination of rhythmic movement an essential part of our education. Moreover, this expression is a part of what you would call our religious ritual. As the poem form in words can suggest deep feeling not possible to the prose form, so it is with the perfect rhythm expressed in the movement of a body dedicated in a dance of worship.

"We also dance sheerly for pleasure as do you, although not exactly in the *manner* of your present-day dancing," she added with a laugh. "We could derive no joy from the kick, wiggle and hop we have observed on your Earth, during which a man and a woman clutch each other ferociously one moment and fling each other off the next. Our social dancing is usually of a group pattern, although often one or more persons, inspired by the moment or the music, will dance for the rest of us. You have seen fine interpretive dancers on your Earth and therefore know the pleasure it is to watch beautiful movement of a body that is inspired by the spirit within."

"We also have parties," Ilmuth said, "although we do not think of them in such terms. With us it is quite simply a matter of inviting our friends to our homes that we may talk or relax together. Many of these are outdoor affairs -- on our beaches or in our gardens. Like yours, many of our homes have grounds that are planned with swimming pools and large terraces." I wished that I need never leave these wonderful people. But at just this point, Ramu rose and said, "It's bad news, but I fear that I must now return you to Earth."

I stood up and tried to bury my regret under the thought of a "next time."

Farewells were said amidst an atmosphere of gaiety and references to another meeting for us all.

No one reminded me to remember all I had been told, nor to apply it properly in my activities on Earth. I was left only with a last impression of beauty and warmth and friendliness, and with the knowledge that once ignorance was lifted from them, the people of my world, too, could grow into the natural heritage of all mankind.

As we reached the door leading out into the control room, I paused to look back that I might again imprint on my mind every detail of this lovely room, my friends and, above all, the radiant portrait of Ageless Life.

--()--

The little Scout had been charged while we were visiting and was now in readiness for our return to Earth. The door was open and together we entered, Ramu, Firkon and I. Ramu went to the controls. The clamp and cable had been removed as we climbed the stairs and, as before, the door silently closed after the last man had entered.

Slowly, we slid down the sloping rail, through two air locks and out again into space through the bottom of the ship. As we descended on the rail, I felt again that sensation of dropping in the pit of my stomach, though it was less intense and of shorter duration than when we entered.

It seemed an impossibly short time before the door slid open and Firkon said, "Here we are again -- back to Earth!"

This time the craft was not set down upon the ground, but remained hovering about six inches above it.

Ramu came forward and extended his hand in farewell, saying, "I shall not be driving in with you as I must remain with the Scout. I am glad of this evening with you and look forward to another soon.

I echoed his sentiments!

The drive back to the hotel was a silent one, full of feeling and deep thoughts on my part. Firkon undoubtedly knew this.

He stopped the car in front of my hotel but did not get out. We shook hands and he said, "We shall be meeting again before long."

I was wondering when and where and he answered the unspoken question by saying, "Do not doubt that you will be alerted at the right time, and find yourself in the right place."

I stepped out of the car. Raising his hand in farewell, Firkon drove away, leaving me standing there on the sidewalk alone

Entering the hotel, I went to my room. For the first time since leaving with my friends, I looked at my watch. It was 5:10 A.M.!

I was not in the least sleepy, nor was I aware of any fatigue. I sat on the edge of the bed for a full hour reviewing the experiences of the night. And even as they went through my mind I could not help but reflect on how fantastic the whole thing would seem to my fellow man.

Nevertheless, I must tell of it. . . .

Actually, I myself could scarcely believe in the reality of all that had happened in the past few hours. Yet I knew what my eyes had seen and my ears had heard, and that without doubt it had been a completely physical experience.

Finally slipping out of my clothes, I stretched out and must have fallen into a light sleep. It was close to eight o'clock when I awakened. I dressed hastily for there was little time left in which to eat breakfast and catch the bus on which I was to return home.

Riding along in the bus, my physical eyes saw the Earthly scenery through which we were passing, and some of the people seated in my immediate vicinity. But my mind, absorbed in the experiences of the previous night, was still traveling space, or with my companions in the giant carrier ship.

The feeling of being in two places simultaneously persisted for several weeks. I found it very difficult to return to the bondage of Earthly ways. Although the time in which I had been privileged to view the vastness of space and the beauty of its constant action had been short, I carried the wonder of it with me. All that I had learned from these friends of other worlds was not given to me alone, but for the sharing with all on Earth willing to receive it.

--()--

CHAPTER 7

THE SCOUT FROM SATURN

Time slipped by with no more meetings with my friends from other worlds. Yet often I felt that they were near.

It was two months later, on April 21st, that I again felt a sudden urge to go to the city. Accordingly, the next day I arranged to be driven to Oceanside, where I caught an early afternoon bus for Los Angeles, which brought me into that city a little more than two hours later.

I registered in the same hotel as before and went to my room to freshen up after my trip. Then I returned downstairs and went into the cocktail lounge for a little chat with my friend, the bar attendant. Shortly after, I returned to the lobby, bought a weekly news magazine and settled down to wait.

This time, the feeling of uncertainty and inner restlessness which had plagued me on the first occasion was entirely absent. I knew the meaning of the urge which had brought me down from the mountains!

So I read with interest the reports on both home and foreign events as printed, plus a bit of what is called "reading between the lines" on my own. Except for the entrance of two men whom I knew slightly, and who came over to exchange a few words, there were no interruptions.

Suddenly I looked up, and there stood my Martian friend, Firkon!

I jumped to my feet with what probably could be described only as a broad grin. Firkon too wore a wide smile, and we exchanged the customary greeting. Then he said a certain word, stressing it in a way which clearly gave to it some particular significance.

As we left the hotel together, he said, "The handclasp has been described to a certain extent and we thought it best to add the word you have just heard as a further identification between you and those of our worlds who are contacting you here. This will be particularly useful in case you are approached by someone strange to you, as will sometimes be the case.

"An excellent precaution," I agreed. Then, glancing at my wrist watch and noting that it was already 7:15.

I said, "If your plans permit, and you would like something to eat, I know of a little café close by where we can sit in a booth and talk undisturbed."

"That will fit in perfectly," he said, adding with a smile, "after all, the body too has to be nourished!"

As we walked along I asked about Ramu. Firkon told me that he would not be with us tonight.

The café was full but we were fortunate in arriving just in time to slip into a booth as the former occupants were leaving. We exchanged greetings with the waitress who came to clear the table. Firkon glanced briefly at the menu she had given him, then laid it aside and ordered a peanut butter sandwich on whole wheat, black coffee and a piece of apple pie.

"I'll take the same," I said.

When we were left alone, he began speaking quietly. "I see that, reading along in that magazine, you were struck by the volume of suspicion, antagonism and hatred which groups of men on your Earth are continuously fostering against other groups.

Since I had not been consciously thinking of this after Firkon's arrival, I was somewhat amazed that he was aware of my reaction.

"Quite simple," he explained, "it is still a very powerful thought picture in what you might call the 'back of your mind.' Few people," he went on, "recognize those destructive emotions within themselves for what they are -- even those who pride themselves on possessing mild dispositions. Yet notice what a small incident is necessary to cause a man to lose his temper. While, with a little more aggravation, he enters the fighting stage and becomes aggressive in what he calls 'self-protection.'

"Actually, this is nothing but a state of emotional unbalance that carries with it a force of fury that sheds all reason. Once recognized, such habit patterns can be curbed, or even broken entirely."

At this point our food was brought. As we were left alone again he continued, "Responsibility for the state of affairs existing on Earth today cannot be blamed on only a few in any nation. In my business and social contacts with my Earth brothers I have encountered many saturated with these destructive emotions and encased in egotism. Naturally, fear and confusion are prevalent. A few have succeeded in developing a higher consideration for their fellow men by seeking to learn more of the universal laws.

Some have chosen the channels of what you call 'metaphysics,' 'occultism' and other similar names. But amongst these there is often a selfish motive toward self-promotion and personal gain rather than the universal motive of service and mutual welfare.

"As a result of such general self-seeking, it makes little difference whom the people may choose as leaders, even if selected from their own ranks. Leaders are subject to the habits of the majority where the majority is in power.

"We of other worlds who have been living unrecognized amongst you can see clearly how identity with Divine origin has been lost. People of Earth have become separate entities which are no longer truly human in expression as in the beginning they were. Now they are but slaves of habit. Nonetheless, imprisoned within these habits is still the original soul that yearns for expression according to its Divine inheritance. This smothered urge is bound to disturb deeply the man chained to his ruts by the mechanism of habit. And this is why, desiring finer and greater expression, more often than men realize, something stirring within the depths of their beings leaves the habit-bound self uneasy and restless. Yet the habit is so powerful in its accumulation that while man wants to listen to this kind, wise voice, he fears to yield, not knowing where it might lead him. However, until man can cast off the shackles of his personal self-pride and allow this voice to guide him, he will continue to live as a warrior against the laws of his own being.

"As you know, so long as men do not desire to change their way of living, none can help them. Those few on Earth who do sincerely desire to learn the laws of the Infinite One must try to lead the others. And we of other worlds will help them."

We had lingered over our meal while Firkon talked. Now he rose from the booth. Outside again, we walked about two blocks to where the same Pontiac was parked at the curb.

It was a blustery night, but I scarcely noticed the storm. During the first part of our journey, my mind was revolving around what Firkon had been saying. Toward the end, I could think only of what new adventures might be mine tonight. The drive from the city seemed shorter this time to the point where, as before, we suddenly turned off the main highway. This time we drove only a short distance before the car stopped.

At first I could make out nothing except the outline of a few low hills to my right and, as far as I could see in the darkness, level terrain in all other directions. Although I felt certain that it was intended we should meet the Scout again, I could see no sign of it, nor any light that might reveal its presence. However, my companion seemed sure of his direction and we walked along for quite some time before the low hills came to a sudden end. There, in the distance, I could make out a gentle glow. My anticipation increased as we set off toward this light and, after about a quarter of a mile or so, the familiar outline of the Scout became visible.

But something was different. This was much larger than the little craft I had in my memory. This one must have been over one hundred feet in diameter, with larger portholes and a much flatter dome. (*Compare illustration numbered 2 with that numbered 9. -- Editor*)

A figure was standing silhouetted against the glow of the ship whom at first I took to be my Venusian friend, wearing the now familiar ski-type pilot's suit. But this pilot proved to be a stranger, a handsome man about six feet tall. He came forward a few steps and greeted us in a warm and friendly manner while giving the usual handclasp. I shall call him Zuhl.

I was wondering if this enormous Saucer was a Martian craft when the pilot corrected my thought by saying, "This Scout is from Saturn, and it too is carried in a large carrier or mother ship such as the one you have already been in."

He turned, led us to the waiting Saucer, whose door was already open, and entered. I followed, Firkon behind me.

This ship was at least four times the diameter of the Venusian Scout and about twice as high -- possibly a little more. The door closed in the same silent way behind Firkon. Instantly the light within increased and the low humming became audible as the machinery started. I felt a slight tug or jerk, not enough to unbalance me, and I guessed that we had left the Earth. As I gazed around, trying to take stock of my new surroundings, the Saturnian pilot explained that this ship was not only larger than the little Scout, but differed in other respects. It had not been hovering above the ground, but was set down firmly on its huge three-ball undercarriage. What I had felt was the jerk necessary to make the break with Earth. Zuhl gave, as an analogy, a piece of iron clinging to a magnet. A jerk takes place at the instant of separation.

As I looked around, I saw the familiar bluish-white diffused light and the same kind of glassy translucent metal walls. On either side was a curved passage about four feet wide, which appeared to encircle the ship. On the outer wall of this passage I noticed a group of portholes, considerably larger than those in the small ship and, from what I could see, I judged there must be four such groups in all, one group in each quadrant.

Ahead, a corridor of the same apparent width, with high walls that reached up into the dome, ran straight forward for about one-third of the ship's diameter. Beyond this there seemed to be a central chamber in which I could see a large magnetic pole placed through the center of the ship.

The pilot then asked me if I would care to go on a tour of the Scout while it was in flight. Needless to say, I would! Leading the way, Zulu took me into the central chamber -- an amazing sight! It is difficult to describe anything so unfamiliar and complicated after seeing it for the first time. However, I shall do my best.

In plan, the ship resembled a wheel. The four corridors were like four spokes leading to the hub or central chamber in which we now stood. The walls ranged twenty to thirty feet from floor to ceiling. They were covered almost entirely by illuminated graphs and charts, over which lines and geometric shapes wove the intricate patterns in continually changing colors that had fascinated me in the Venusian Scout. Beautiful to watch, these held me equally enthralled, although I could understand them no better.

About halfway up around the circular walls ran a delicate metal balcony, reached by a ladder. Above the walls was the translucent dome itself, surmounted by an enormous telescopic lens. Almost the entire floor space was taken up by an equally gigantic lens, at least twice the diameter of the one in the Venusian ship. Around this were four curved benches on which observers could sit and gaze down through space at the planet beneath. But the central magnetic pole, running from floor to dome, dominated the entire chamber. This huge silent rod of power, passing through the two great lenses, contained the secrets we yearn for -- the secrets of interplanetary fight.

As I have indicated, the ship was divided into four quadrants by the four radial corridors. These corridors entered the central chamber by four openings. Turning to our left, we now walked along one of the corridors.

About halfway down its length we came upon two large archways opposite each other in the corridor walls. The pilot led me through the right-hand arch into a part of the ship which he described as the crew's sleeping quarters. This whole quadrant was divided in an interesting manner. In front of us were about a dozen small private rooms or cubicles where each member of the crew had his private sleeping place. I did not go into any of them, but as all the doors were open, I was able to see how perfectly and compactly they were equipped -- in a manner our Pullman engineers might envy!

A kind of ship's ladder with handrails ran up to a section immediately over the sleeping quarters. This, I believe, was the only part of the ship to contain two complete decks within one quadrant. Up here was a kind of dormitory or restroom, equipped with couches and deep comfortable chairs where the crew could rest or converse. The ceiling of this apartment was formed entirely by the slope of the translucent dome, and it reminded me of a dream-like solarium. Certainly it must have been a lovely way of relaxing, under the huge curved glassy dome with stars and space out beyond.

While taking all this in, I wondered how many crew members there were. "Normally twelve men comprise a full crew," said Zulu, "but at the moment there are only two men on board beside myself, since no more are necessary for a short trip like this."

Then I wondered whether all the members of this particular crew were Saturnians, since it was a Saturnian ship. This thought was corrected when Zulu said, "Although this Scout was built on Saturn, no particular planet owns it. Instead, we share it. Consequently, its crew has members from all planets.

"As you can see, this is a large Scout and designed for long-range travel. It can remain away from its mother ship for a week or more without having to return for recharge, as it carries generating equipment on board which serves this purpose. In case of emergency, additional power for a recharge can also be beamed direct to any Saucer from the mother ship."

When we stood in the hallway near the sleeping quarters, I fancied I noticed a faint vibration under my feet. I understood why when Zulu explained, "Most of the machinery is installed directly under the floor in this section. There is also a machine shop that can be entered directly from the sleeping quarters." I looked for a door but saw none, which did not surprise me.

As we again came out into the corridor, I glanced through the arch that led into the next quadrant. I saw a soft blaze of colored lights and strange instruments -- the control room itself. There were two young men sitting at control panels. We continued along until we had reached the outer circular corridor.

--()--

Illustrations

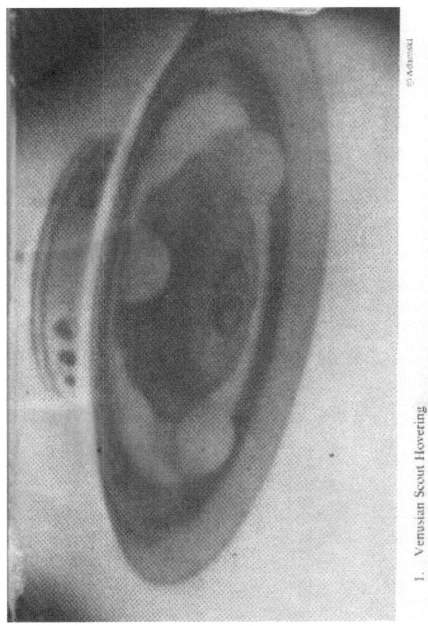

Above - 1. Venusian Scout Hovering

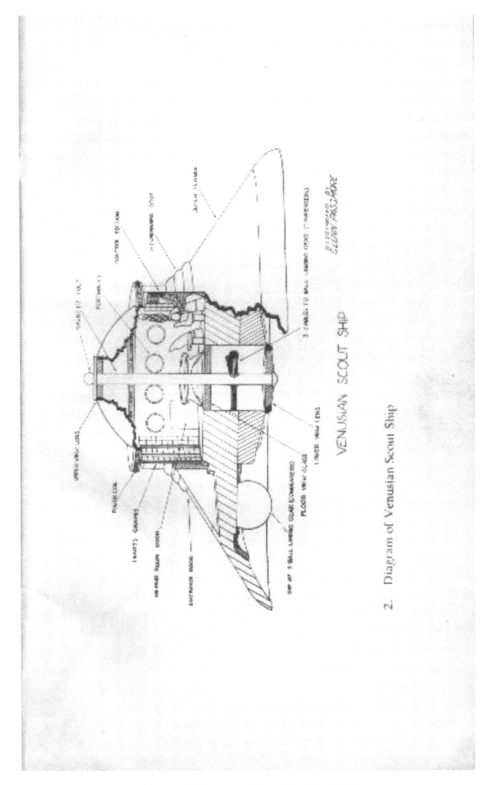

Above - 2. Diagram of Venusian Scout Ship

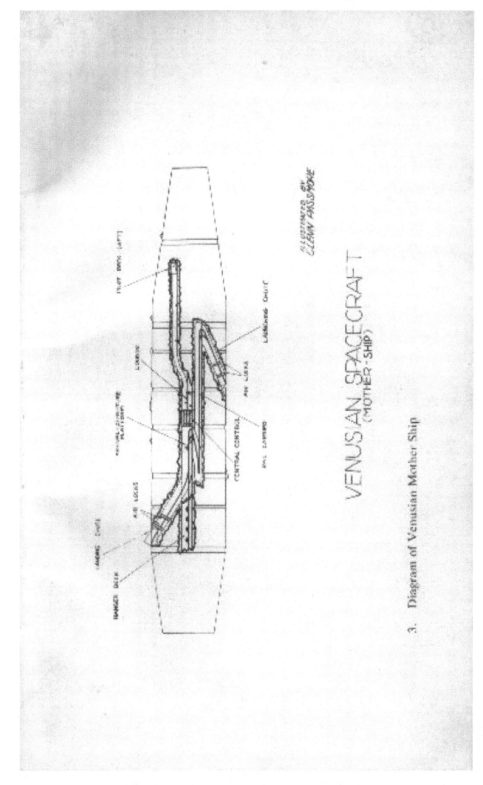

Above - 3. Diagram of Venusian Mother Ship

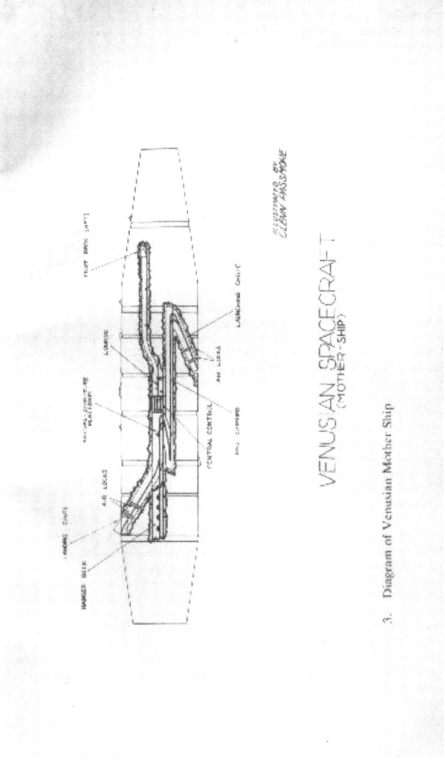

Above - 3. Diagram of Venusian Mother Ship

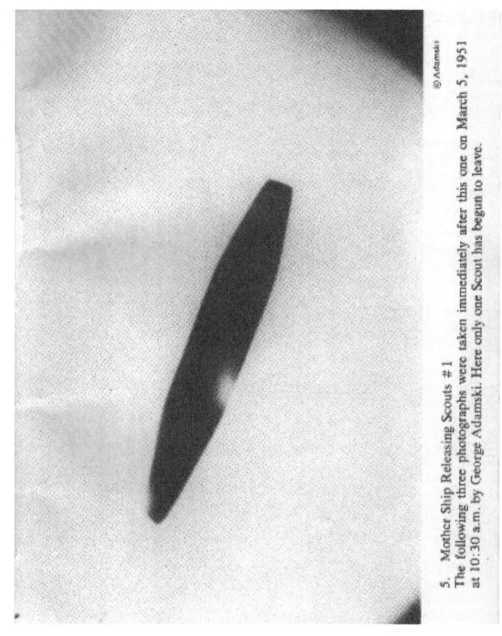

Above - 5. Mother Ship Releasing Scouts #1

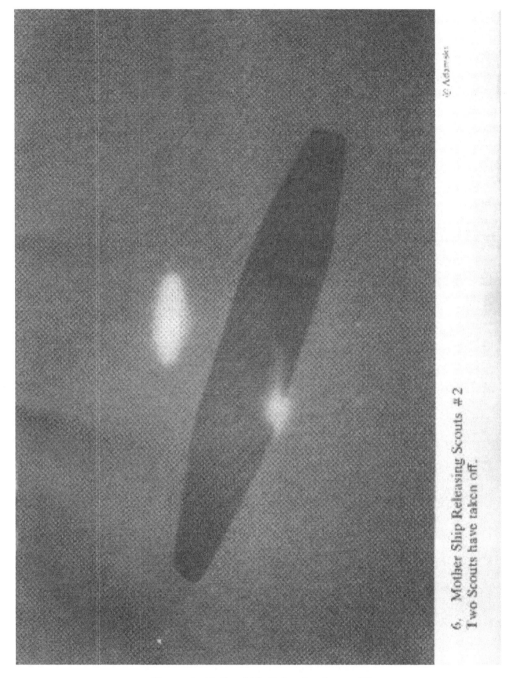

Above - 6. Mother Ship Releasing Scouts #2

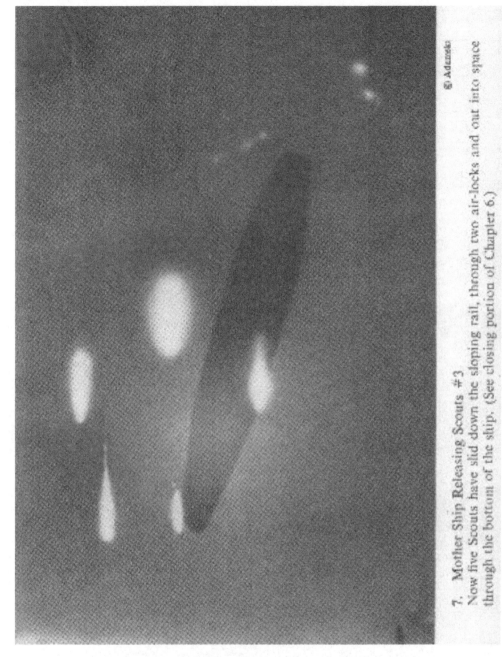

Above - 7. Mother Ship Releasing Scouts #3

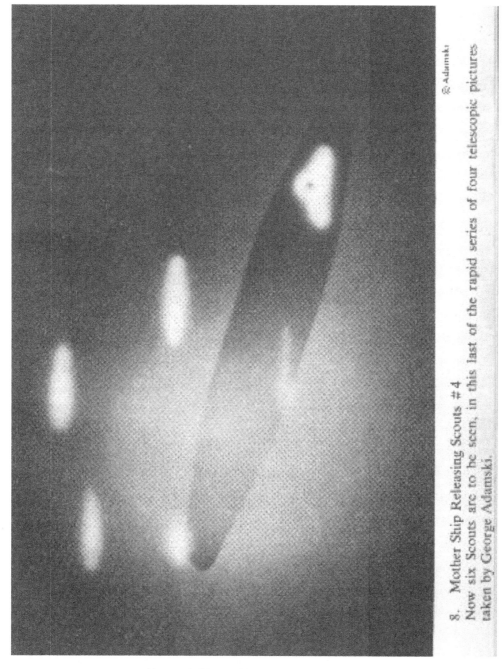

Above - 8. Mother Ship Releasing Scouts #4

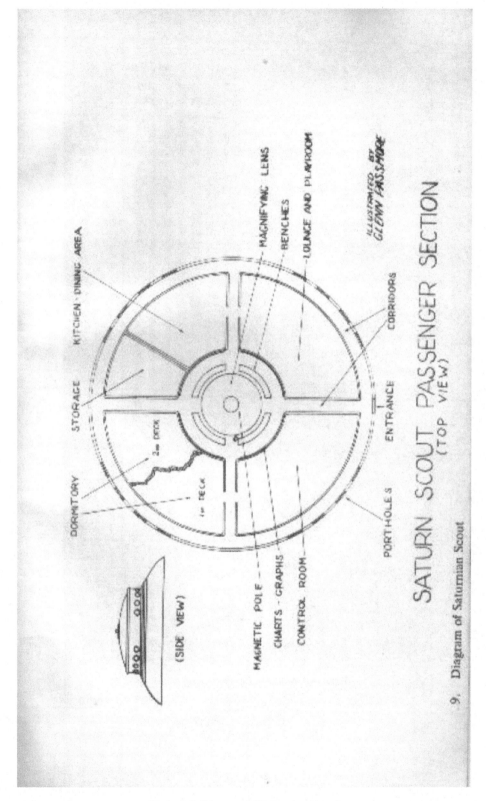

Above - 9. Diagram of Saturnian Scout

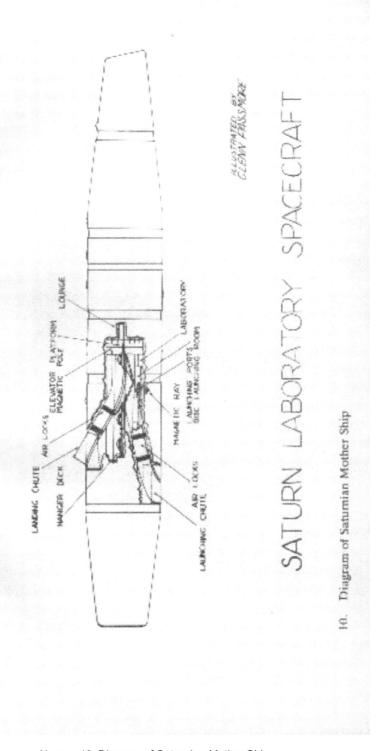

Above - 10. Diagram of Saturnian Mother Ship

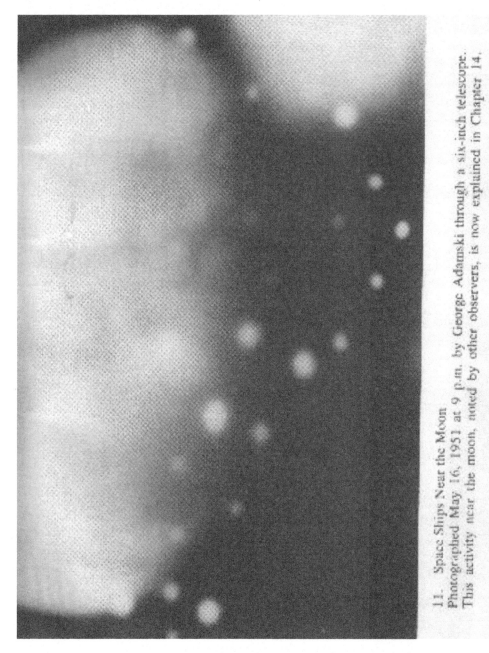

Above - 11. Space Ships Near the Moon

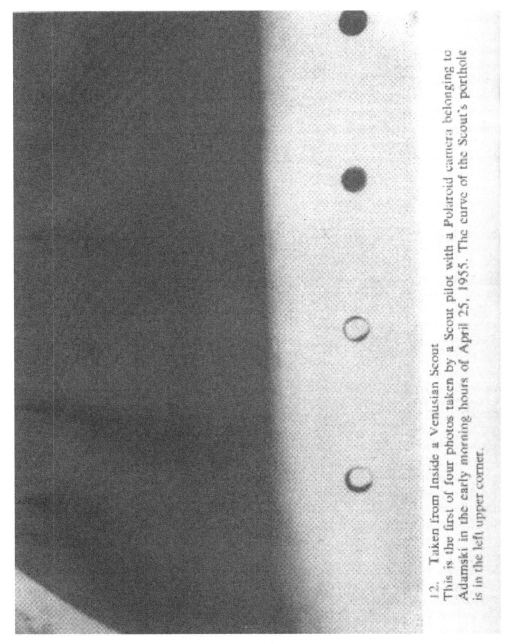

Above - 12. Taken from Inside a Venusian Scout

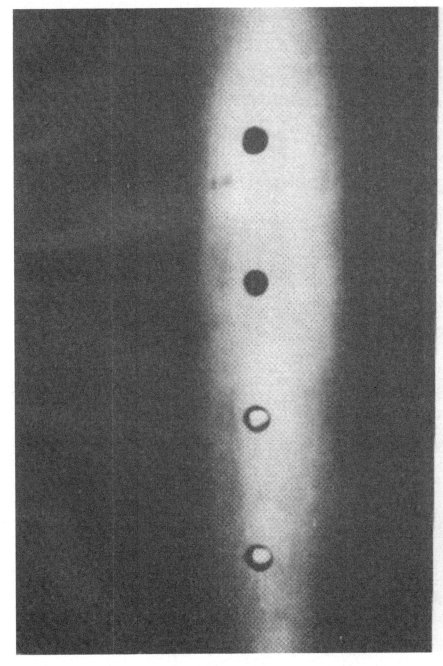

Above - 13. Portholes of a Small Mother Ship

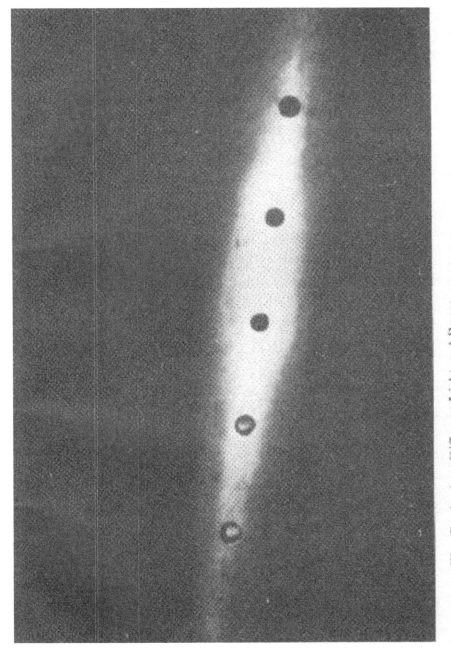

Above - 14. The Carrier in a different Light and Range

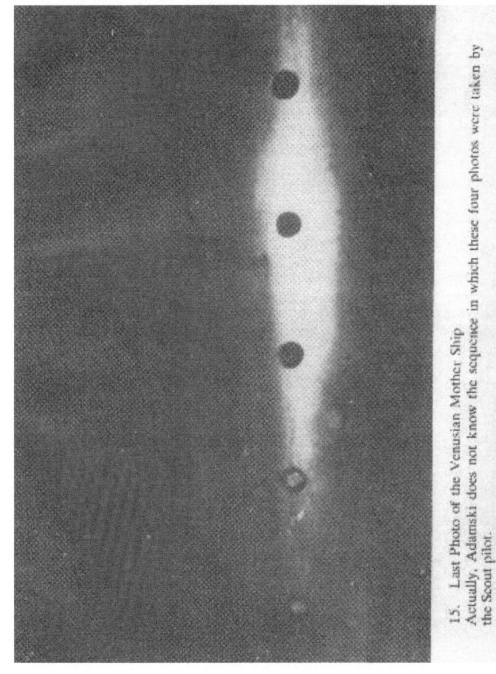

Above - 15. Last Photo of the Venusian Mother Ship

16. George Adamski
A recent snapshot taken at his home on the slopes of Mount Palomar. In the background is the observatory housing his fifteen-inch telescope.

Above - 16. George Adamski

--()--

We turned right and Zuhl said, "In this room is a compartment where we keep two small, remotely controlled, 'registering disks.' These are what we send out for close observation work. Highly sensitive instruments, they transmit their findings not only to the Scout, but also direct to the mother ship so that duplicate records can be made. One set goes into the permanent records on one of the planets for the use of anyone requiring that particular information. These little disks have contributed much to our knowledge of the conditions on Earth, throughout the whole solar system and even in systems beyond."

Walking along the outer corridor as our tour continued, we passed a group of four large portholes but did not stop to look out.

When we arrived at the next radial corridor, we again turned right and began making our way back to the ship's center between two solid-looking walls of the same translucent material. These walls were very thick and strong, and formed an integral structural feature, as do the spokes of a wheel. I could see that the wall on my right must be the rear wall of the sleeping quarters. And Zuhl explained that the opposite wall contained the entrance to a rather large storage compartment stocked with food and other supplies for an extended trip.

As the pilot mentioned the words "extended trip" I wondered if this ship could travel between planets without the aid of a carrier ship. This he disproved, stating that the Scouts are not built for traveling in outer space.

Once more we entered the central chamber with its flashing, mobile wall graphs. We skirted the central lens and left by the third radial corridor, the last still to be explored. As in its counterpart opposite, this corridor also had two large arches leading off from its midway point. First we turned and went through the left-hand arch into a room which I was told was their kitchen. But I would never have guessed this, for it bore very little resemblance to anything we know as a kitchen. It appeared as an almost bare room with plain walls. But the appearance proved deceptive. Zuhl told me that these walls were lined from top to bottom with cupboards and compartments which, like all doors in these amazingly constructed craft, were invisible until opened. In these cupboards food and everything necessary for its preparation were stored.

A small glass-like door was set into one of the walls leading into what he said was an oven. When I looked in and saw no burners of any description, Zulu explained, "We do not cook our food in the same way as you. Ours is done quickly by means of rays or high frequencies, a method with which you are now experimenting on Earth. However, we prefer most of our food in the state in which it is grown, and live chiefly on the delicious fruits and vegetables which abound on our planets. To all intents and purposes we are what you call 'vegetarians,' but in emergencies, if no other food is available, we do eat meat."

I realized later that I had seen no sinks, garbage or plumbing arrangements but, since I am no housewife, I did not register their absence at the time. But undoubtedly such facilities must have existed, probably as mysteriously superior to ours as was everything else. Nor did I see any chairs, tables or benches. No doubt, whatever was necessary was tucked away between the walls.

We left this kitchen and entered a lounge fully as luxurious as the beautiful one in the Venusian carrier, where couches and single seats in several styles were scattered about. In comfortable proximity were the same kind of occasional tables with transparent tops. On these were beautiful little ornaments. Zulu said that the crew members whiled away many hours in this room during observation trips through the atmosphere of whatever planet they might be studying. He also explained that, even as Earth men, they played many games, which they thoroughly enjoyed, and also entertained guests here.

I saw no books, papers or reading matter of any kind, nor did I see any shelves or cases in which something of this kind might be kept. But I do not question that such things were present.

The floor-covering in this room, as well as throughout the ship, was yellow-gray in color. There was no particular design in it and although the surface appeared very firm, it felt similar to thick sponge rubber as I walked on it.

We stopped only a moment in this inviting lounge. Returning to the center corridor, we continued on to the first one by which we had entered the Scout.

Although so much had been shown and explained to me in this fascinating craft, I was not allowed more than a quick glance into the control room, and no explanation was given concerning the power that operated any of the mechanical equipment. While I knew that they traveled by utilizing the natural forces in space, transformed into motivating power, I did not understand the *how,* and admit I was hoping for information.

But with an almost apologetic smile, Zulu told me that they still could not fully trust any Earth man to the extent of revealing certain things. "For," he said, "you on Earth have not yet learned control of your emotions, which often causes you to speak before you think. In so doing, you could be led into giving information unwisely to an unworthy mind who might pervert its use.

I could not deny the truth of this.

Our journey through the Scout had been a rapid one, and explanations were given en route. In spite of this, we had scarcely completed our tour when Zulu announced, "We have reached our carrier and are ready to enter."

Although they did not tell me how far out we were, I had a definite feeling that this carrier was much farther from Earth than the Venusian ship had been. Neither could I watch the entrance of our craft into the larger one, as we were close to the center of the Scout with no view out. Yet in many ways there was a feeling of likeness to the former experience, although at the same time a difference which I was unable to explain.

As we lowered into the interior of the waiting craft there was again the sensation of dropping in an elevator, but no feeling of losing balance.

When the Scout came to a standstill on its rails and the door was opened onto a platform as in the other carrier, no one was there to meet us and attach clamps over the flange and the rail as had been done on the Venusian ship for the smaller Scout.

Stepping out of this Scout and onto the platform within this carrier from Saturn, I immediately sensed that this ship was different in almost every respect from the Venusian carrier. I wondered what adventures awaited me here, but at no time had I the least sense of fear. *(See illustration numbered 10 and compare with that numbered 3. -- Editor)*

Indeed, each fresh meeting with these people of other worlds served but to make any part of fear an utter absurdity. At all times I have felt very humble for the privilege

which has been granted me to listen to their words of wisdom and to visit and travel in their beautiful ships. All that they have asked of me is that I pass their knowledge on to my fellow man, whoever and wherever he may be. This I shall do, leaving to each man the privilege of believing or disbelieving, of benefiting from a higher knowledge, or casting it aside in derision and skepticism.

--()--

CHAPTER 8

THE SATURNIAN MOTHER SHIP

What I shall attempt to describe is rather complex. Most of the mechanical arrangements I saw after boarding the Saturnian mother ship were entirely new to me. At first I could not fully comprehend their functions, but later I was helped to some understanding of them.

The platform beside which we had stopped (I say "platform," but actually it proved to be a magnetic elevator some fifty feet square) carried people and freight from the bottom to the top of this gigantic carrier ship through an enormous shaft two hundred feet or more in depth. A magnetic pole rose the full height of this shaft, passing through the center of the elevator and, I learned, provided the power and means by which it operated.

This was the first thing -- this and the great shaft rising upward -- that struck me on alighting from the Saucer. Ahead of us was a kind of bridge with side rails that connected the elevator platform to the deck where our Saucer had stopped, for the fifty-foot platform did not completely fill the width of the shaft. This puzzled me at first.

As Zuhl and I walked on, I turned and gazed around me, awed by the majesty and superb construction of this colossal ship. Looking back, I could see, high up above and beyond the dome of our Saucer, the ceiling of the immense chamber through which we had descended. A large set of rails sloped upward and through this ceiling, continuing somewhere in the heights above where the airlocks must have been. I could look straight on up to the opening in the mother ship through which we had just come.

As we reached the platform, Firkon suggested that I look into the elevator shaft. I did so and saw three more floors or deck levels above, and three below, making a total of seven. At each level a bridge or balcony-extension projected into the shaft to cover the gap between the edge of the platform and the deck proper. These extensions, I later learned, can be raised like drawbridges.

In length they are equal to the height of the deck from floor to ceiling, so that when raised they obscure the deck entrance, making a smooth side to the shaft and completely sealing it off from the rest of the ship. When the elevator platform arrives at its destination, this portion of the shaft wall hinges downward until it becomes the projecting balcony. When this takes place, the handrails on the elevator swing outward and form handrails for the balcony. When the elevator moves onward, these rails swing back from the balcony and form a guard rail on the elevator.

I saw how these rails operated just after leaving the Scout. As soon as we had crossed the balcony and stepped onto the elevator, the side rails closed in behind us, even though we were not going to ascend. While I was gazing around, trying to take in every detail, Zulu stopped by a small control panel which was raised about four inches from the floor of the elevator, probably to prevent anyone from stepping upon it accidentally. This panel was about thirty inches long and somewhere between six to eight inches wide. On it were six buttons staggered in two rows for easy operation by the feet. Each button was marked to indicate its purpose.

But I could neither read nor understand these markings.

Zuhl stepped on one of the buttons, and immediately the railings on the other side of the platform swung outward and took up a new position as guard rails for the balcony extension on the far side of the shaft which we had now reached. Simultaneously, a beautifully proportioned and ornamented door in the wall before us slid open, revealing to me yet another wonderful sight.

We were now in an exquisite salon, very similar in furnishing and design to the one in the Venusian carrier, though somewhat larger. Once again it was beautifully illuminated by the same mysterious soft light without obvious source. However, my attention was almost immediately arrested by six women and six men who apparently were awaiting our arrival. They had been sitting in a close group, conversing amongst themselves. As we entered, they arose and smiled. A man and a woman came forward to greet us, including rue warmly although I had never met them before.

The women were dressed in beautiful, sheer gowns made of material that seemed to radiate an almost living quality. Each had a wide belt apparently part of the garment itself, decorated with gems that sparkled with a softness and vitality such as I had never seen in any gem on Earth.

These jeweled belts are the only ornament that I have ever seen worn by women of other worlds. And as I marveled at these gems, I found myself wondering if, rather than being superior in themselves to those of Earth, [that] their extraordinary brilliance might not result from the radiance of their wearers -- a thought later verified by Firkon.

The ladies' gowns had long, full sleeves, drawn together at the wrists. The necklines were cut round. Although differing in color according to each lady's choice, all were of soft pastel shades which lent to the entire group an aspect of harmonious charm.

In height, the women ranged from a little under five feet to about five feet, eight inches. All were slender and beautifully formed. Their features were delicate and their faces lovely in contour. In coloring, every type was represented, from complexions very fair with a faint rosy tinge to soft, smooth olive. The ears were small; the eyes large and very expressive under brows beautiful in line. The mouths of all seemed to be of average size with natural red lips, varying in deepness of color with skin tones.

All wore their hair shoulder length, loosely yet charmingly arranged. Both men and women wore sandals. None of the women looked to be more than in their early twenties. Later, Firkon told me that their ages ranged from thirty to two hundred years! While the loose, flowing gowns revealed merely a suggestion of the perfect symmetry of their bodies, when later they changed into close-fitting uniforms, the beauty and grace with which all were formed became clearly apparent.

The men wore gleaming white blouses, open wide at the throat, with long full sleeves drawn in tight at the wrists, somewhat similar to those worn by men of the eighteenth century on Earth. The trousers were also loose, very similar to our own styles. But the material had a softness and a texture unlike anything I had ever seen.

The men's height varied from about five to six feet, and all were splendidly formed, with weight in proportion. Like the women, they varied in coloring, but I noticed that the skin of one was definitely what we would call copper-colored. All had neatly trimmed hair, although it differed in length and cut to some degree, as here on Earth. None wore long hair as did Orthon, my Venusian friend of the first meeting. I have since learned that he had a particular reason for wearing his hair in this style.

The men's features, though uniformly handsome, were not greatly different from those of Earth men, and I am positive that any one of them could come amongst us and never be recognized as not belonging here. None looked older than somewhere in the early thirties, but this impression was also corrected later by Firkon, who told me that their ages ranged from forty to several hundred years according to our scale on Earth.

Immediately after the greetings, we were invited to be seated around a large oval table, on which were goblets filled with a clear liquid. Like all I had seen, this table had a transparent top, slightly different from either glass or any kind of plastic known on Earth. It had no covering, nor was it etched, carved or decorated in any way. There was an indescribable beauty about the material itself which needed no ornamentation.

The chairs drawn up to it were styled much like our dining-room chairs. There were fifteen of these, corresponding to the number of persons present.

As we seated ourselves -- I between Zulu and Firkon -- we were invited to drink the liquid in the goblets. Al-though as clear in appearance as our purest water, the flavor was similar to natural apricot juice; sweet and slightly heavy, entirely delicious.

Although the methods by which these space travelers were able to learn any language spoken on Earth had all been explained to me, this facility still held an element of surprise.

The lady who had first come forward to greet us as we entered started the conversational ball rolling as she said, "This ship is a scientific laboratory. We travel space solely for the purpose of studying the constant changes taking place within space itself. We observe the life and conditions on the many planets we encounter as we move through space. Naturally, learning the different languages is a necessity. It is through the research made by ships like ours that space travel has been developed to the present degree of safety. Something of this was explained to you on the ship from Venus, but there you were not shown how the instruments are operated. On this ship,' however, you will see our instruments in operation, and we shall explain some of their functions to you that you may gain a greater understanding of how we have learned to use the natural forces."

She then went on to explain that this ship too belonged to no one planet, but was a universal ship, manned by people from many planets and operated for the welfare and knowledge of all.

"On this particular trip," she explained, "three of the women are inhabitants of the planet you call Mars, and the other three from Venus. Usually, there are also three Saturnian women who, for certain reasons, could not join us on this trip. So Saturn is represented only by her men. Occasionally, men and women from solar systems even beyond our own join the crew of this and other ships of the same type. In every case, crew members are highly trained by our most advanced scientists."

Almost as though there had been no interruption in the discussion between Firkon and myself earlier in the evening, the subject of the problems facing inhabitants of our world was resumed here, around this beautiful table. As usual, the absence of condemnation or harsh judgment of any kind was remarkable. Instead, an understanding sympathy for the suffering of the people of Earth was apparent throughout.

One of the Martian ladies said, "You Earth people do not desire to show such cruelty toward one another. This, as you have been told before, is merely the result of your self-ignorance, which in turn blinds you to the laws of the Universe of which we are all a part.

"Within your families, you speak much of the love you feel for one another. Yet this very love you profess to hold often expresses itself as a possessive power of bondage over another. Nothing could be more contrary to love in its free state. Genuine love must embrace respect, mutual confidence and understanding. As known and expressed on other worlds, love contains nothing of the false possessiveness which perverts it upon the Earth.

"We understand love as a radiation from the heart of Deity through all creation, and especially through man toward all other forms, without division of any kind. In reality, it is not possible to find virtue in one form, and none in another.

"Yet, notice the distortion existing on Earth, solely because man there understands neither himself nor his Divine Father. Because of this ignorance, men go forth in what you call 'war' to slaughter ruthlessly those of another nation, another color, another religion, without understanding what they do. It is difficult for us of other worlds to grasp why men of Earth cannot see that not only is the mutual destruction of themselves by themselves no answer to any problem, but a cause for further woe on Earth. So it has always been and so it will always be. Now that your scientific knowledge has so far outstripped your social and human progress, the gap between *must* be filled with urgent haste. Men of your Earth *know* the terrible power sealed within the bombs they are piling up for use against one another. Yet they blunder on ever nearer to the brink of an unthinkable world-wide slaughter. This, to us, is strangely illogical."

"Yes," one of the men agreed, "your behavior does often seem illogical to us. Let me give you an example. You have physical fathers on Earth, do you not?"

"Yes," I replied.

"If you had two sons, born of your own flesh and blood, as you say, and if for one reason or another one of your Sons knelt before you and asked your blessing on his determination to slay his brother, who is also your son, would-you grant his request because he professed himself right and his brother wrong?"

My reply was naturally, "Of course not!"

"Yet," he pointed out, "that is exactly what you Earthlings have been doing throughout the centuries. You all acknowledge a Supreme Being according to your understanding, and you speak of the brotherhood of mankind. Yet you ask the Eternal Father of all things to do that which you yourselves would not do. For when you people are warring against one another, you fall to your knees in unholy prayer. You ask your Divine Father to bless your efforts to gain a victory over your own life brother, even to the extent of destroying him.

"We, as your brothers living on other worlds than your own, view impartially the divided groups of people upon your planet. We, who have learned more regarding our Father's laws, operative throughout the Universe, cannot make the distinctions that keep you in such constant turmoil and we are saddened to see what is taking place on your Earth. We, as brothers of all mankind, are willing to help all those whom we can reach and who desire our help. But at no time may we force our way of life upon the people of your world.

"In reality, there are no inherently bad people on Earth, nor anywhere in the Universe. If, as many of you express it, your lives seem to consist of a 'hell on Earth,' you yourselves are to blame. Your planet, even as all others, was created by our One Divine Creator and is in itself a holy place, as are all His creations. Were all mankind suddenly to be swept from the face of Earth, and 'with them the strife and woe and grief they have brought upon it by not learning how to live together, Earth would be beautiful. But never so beautiful as a world on which men live as brothers with all in the Universe.

"Because one man is a stranger to another does not give him the right to ignore, insult, or to kill a fellow being.

"You have set aside a day each year for the observance of the Brotherhood of Man, and you speak of the Fatherhood of the Creator. Yet, in complete oblivion of the actions which such declarations should bring forth, you lavish money and effort toward swifter and more widespread ways of maiming and destroying your fellow men on Earth. Does it not seem curious to pray to the Divine Father to bless your efforts in this ruthless destruction?

"We hear these prayers coming from your temples, from your government leaders, from your homes and from the battlefields. Can you not see how far astray you have gone? For you are actually asking your Divine Father to do that which you yourself would not do for your own children. Can you not see how hypocritical you have become? And this is but one illustration of the many things which you do against your Divine Father.

"So long as you live this way, divided one against the other, your sorrows will be multiplied. For when you seek your brother's life, someone seeks yours. This is the meaning of the words once spoken by Jesus of Nazareth. Remember that he said: 'Put up again thy sword into its place: for all they who take the sword shall perish with the sword.' The truth of these words has been proven throughout the history of man on Earth."

As he ceased speaking, a picture of the Earth and the problems of the men thereon flashed before my eyes, and I was saddened for my fellow men and for myself as Earthlings. For with the picture came also the realization of how gigantic is the task to correct these conditions. So many throughout the world are unawakened to the causes behind them. Only when enough people realize what they are and, with their whole hearts, desire to change them by giving up their personal greeds and the desire for exaltation, one above the other, can it come to pass.

No one person, no one nation, no one part of the world could alone be blamed for the conditions that I saw pictured, nor could any one segment of civilization do much to alter it. Responsibility lies with each and every person -- and who can forcibly change another? A bondage that is the result of centuries of accumulated misunderstandings, divisions and personal desire for power is difficult to break.

As this realization filled me, I was overcome with humble gratitude to our Divine Father for permitting His children from other worlds who understood our problems of Earth to come our way and extend helping hands of love and compassion to us. Although they could not force change upon us, nor actively interfere, they could help the receptive amongst us to strive *together* for a better world, instead of warring *against* one another and thus causing further divisions.

I realized that much time must pass before such change could come, for mankind has grown to accept pain and sorrow as inevitable, seldom seeking to deviate from the familiar path.

Emerging from my musings, I noticed that the ladies were rising from their chairs.

"We must now don our pilot suits," a lovely brunette explained, "after which we shall go to the instrument room where you will see many things about which you have wondered."

Their departure gave me an opportunity to observe details of this beautiful salon.

On the wall directly in front of us was a huge chart of the heavens. This showed twelve planets in our system with its central Sun. Surrounding ours were other systems with their suns and planets shown in a way that was new to me. Throughout space, between the planets, were details of the various atmospheric conditions existing in space, of which we on Earth are totally unaware. I was told that this knowledge is very important for safe space traveling. There were many markings on this chart, which I was unable to read, but I figured that the purpose was similar to that of our many road maps used by motorists on Earth for convenience in traveling. This was corroborated by one of the men.

Beyond this huge chart, on the same wall but farther toward the back of the lounge, was a detailed diagram of this ship, and it too was marked with symbols of characters which were entirely unfamiliar to me.

The other walls were covered with landscape scenes of some of the planets which this ship had visited. These were not framed paintings hung on the walls, but were more like murals. There was such a liveliness about them that one felt physically present in every scene depicted. This particular quality was something that I had noticed about all their paintings and portraits. The explanation given me was that, whatever the people of space do, so much of themselves goes into their work that it actually does vibrate with their life-force and the radiance of their personalities.

The landscapes were very much like paintings and photographs of Earthly scenes. They showed mountains, valleys, small running streams and oceans.

I saw that the six women had returned dressed in their pilot suits. As they entered, the men rose from the table, and one of them said, "Now we will go to the laboratory."

We walked together to the elevator that had originally brought us. At our approach, the door slid silently open, although I saw no one touch a button. This could be similar in operation to our present-day photoelectric cell.

The fifteen of us stepped onto the elevator and Zuhl took over its operation. I saw him go to another control panel in the corner opposite the one which I first described. There he stepped on one of the buttons and slowly and silently we began to descend.

As we were lowered below the level of the Scout, which was still where we had left it, I noticed a vast chamber in back of it extending far toward that end of the ship. Through the center of this compartment and at right angles to the elevator shaft was a pair of rails. Resting on these were four other Scouts identical in size and design with the one which had brought us up from Earth. This was apparently the storage hangar where they rested while the huge carrier was in interplanetary flight. Along the outer edge, and slightly below each rail, was a catwalk about six feet in width, with a wall on the outside of the walk.

We passed two other balconies below the one over which we had entered the lounge, and I figured that each of these must lead to another deck in this gigantic carrier. At the third balcony below the one leading to the lounge, the elevator was stopped. Thus, looking up from the bottom of the great shaft I was able to count the seven decks on that side of the ship.

As the elevator came to a smooth stop, the railing swung open. On the way down, I had noticed a pair of rails continuing through the lower front part of the ship. These formed a V-junction with the rails by which our Scout had entered, and I realized that these were the rails down which it would travel when we left the carrier for our return to Earth. This indicated that this whole section of the ship was taken up by arrival and departure tunnels, the main shaft, and the huge hangar deck for the Scouts. Somewhere in the same section, either adjoining or beyond the hangar deck, there was probably a maintenance hangar and repair shop, while beyond that again, at the far end of the ship, I knew there must be a control room and pilot's compartment. I had been told that there was one at each end of these colossal craft. On this side of the ship we were taken into a very large room which proved to be the laboratory.

--()--

CHAPTER 9

THE LABORATORY

Never had I seen anything like this room, packed with the most amazing array of instruments imaginable. Here were rows upon rows of graphs and control panels. It seemed to me that every one of these strange instruments I was viewing for the first time was equipped with its own large control console. Six were already in action, and the six men who had accompanied us from the lounge immediately took their places at six more. There still remained a number untended. I noticed on the left shoulders of four of the men an insignia of some sort.

The woman pilot who stood closest to me said, "All operators of these instruments are what you would call advanced scientists. The shoulder insignia of the four men indicates that they are Saturnians."

As had been the case in every other instance, the graphs here showed colored lights with many types of lines and figures, minus any of the dials or gauges so familiar on Earth. In spite of the number of graphs I had now seen, they were still mysteries to me.

"This is where we test the densities of the atmosphere around the Earth," the woman pilot continued, "or of any planet or body which we approach. We study carefully the combinations of the elements of the atmosphere surrounding each body, as well as the elemental combinations of outer space. Although these are in a constant state of change, there is a pattern of behavior according to universal laws. This causes certain combinations to remain for longer periods of time than others. In observing the activities of space, we are able, among other things, to detect the formation of any new body in outer space and determine its speed of growth."

This was amazing to me, and I would gladly have remained in this room watching and trying to fathom the workings of these instruments -- some of which closely resembled our larger TV sets -- which I hoped might give me some understanding of what the changing patterns were revealing.

But the pilot said, "Now we will go on to something else about which you have been wondering."

She led me across the large laboratory room, Firkon, Zuhl and the women following. Here we began to ascend a sloping ramp that extended the full width of the ship. We continued on up still another ramp which led into a large room.

It seemed that wonders would never cease. Each new step brought fresh marvels until I began to fear that I could not retain half of them in my memory. But my friends assured me that when the time came to write, they would help me to recall an accurate picture of the night's events in every detail. I doubt if many men have spent a night so full of surprises, beauty and vastly instructive sights, sounds and conversation.

Now, to my great excitement, I saw here twelve small disks lined up in two rows on opposite sides of the ship. I guessed immediately that these were the registering disks or small, remotely controlled devices sent out by the mother ships for close observation. They were about three feet in diameter, of shiny, smooth material, and shaped rather like two shallow plates, or hub-caps, turned upside down and joined at the rims so that the central part was a few inches thick. I learned, however, that such disks varied in size from about ten inches to twelve feet in diameter, depending on the amount of equipment carried. As I have stated elsewhere, they contained highly sensitive apparatus which not only guided each little Saucer perfectly in its desired path of flight, but also transmitted back to the mother ship full information on every kind of vibration taking place in the area under observation.

Vibrations cover a large field of waves pertaining to sound, radio, light -- and even thought waves; all of these could be monitored back to the parent craft for recording and analysis. Technically, perhaps, these small disks were the finest feat of interplanetary engineering I had yet seen. For in addition to the functions I have listed, they could also be disintegrated if out of control and in danger of falling to Earth, either rapidly by a kind of explosion or, if life or property on the ground were in danger, by a gradual disintegration process. These little aerial wonders were lined up on a wide table on each side of the room, resting in a kind of groove. In the ship's wall directly behind each disk was an opening like a port or trap door large enough for them to pass through. However, at the time we entered, all were closed.

Forcing my gaze away from them for a moment, I took time out to look around. I noticed that the rails and rail-bed of the Scout exit tunnel came down through the ceiling at the far end of this chamber, continuing downward through the floor. Turning back to the disks, I observed a long control panel built into the front part of the tables that held them.

When we came into the room, no seats had been visible, but as the six women took their places before the control panels small stool-like seats rose silently from the floor, possibly due to pressure on a foot pedal.

These control panels differed slightly from others I had seen, and I cannot be certain whether small buttons were recessed into the panels, or whether they were operated by means of keys like an organ. Once seated, the women worked very quickly, their nimble fingers darting above the instruments as they fed instructions and flight data to the waiting disks. I remember noting the resemblance to six women playing in pantomime, a silent concerto. It was fascinating to see how, when a disk had received full "instructions," one of the trap doors would open and the disk would slide smoothly into the orifice, passing through airlocks before hurtling away into outer space on its mission.

Zulu had remained with Firkon and me, and when I asked where the disks had gone, it was he who said, "Let us return to the laboratory where we can follow their flight on the instrument panels."

On our way back, he mentioned that the mother ship was now under way, but did not reveal our destination. I had been aware of no movement whatsoever, nor had I heard any additional sound.

Back in the laboratory, all the men were still operating the instruments in front of them. I noticed on one of the screens varying lines shaping, disappearing and reappearing in new formations. The lines would then be replaced by round dots and long dashes, which would quickly form into various geometrical figures. At the same time, other screens were showing different colors of changing intensities, some in flashes and others in waves. Figures would form on them from time to time. These, too, changed rapidly in size and shape. Everything was a vast mystery to me.

"The men are registering with their instruments what is taking place on the screens," the Saturnian pilot explained, "all of which will later be made into educational records."

Curiosity prompted me to ask what had become of the two disks which we had watched leave the ship.

The pilot explained, "The disks are now hovering above a certain inhabited spot on Earth and registering the sounds emanating from that spot. This is what you are seeing on the screen as shown by the lines, dots and dashes. The other machines are assembling this information and interpreting it by producing pictures of the meanings of the signals, together with the original sounds."

It must have been obvious that I understood none of it too well for Zuhl further explained, "Everything in the Universe has its own particular pattern. For example, if someone speaks the word 'house,' the mental image of a dwelling of one kind or another is in his mind. Many things, including human emotions, are registered in the same way.

"By the use of these machines, we know even what your people are thinking, and whether or not they are hostile toward us. For if there are harsh, frightening words, or even thoughts, these will picture themselves in that manner and our recorders will pick them up accurately. In the same way, we know who amongst you will prove friendly and receptive. Everything in the entire Universe moves by 'vibration,' as you have called it on Earth -- or, more recently, 'frequencies.' It is by these frequencies or vibrations that we learn the languages of other worlds."

During his explanation, I watched the screens and the ever-changing patterns. I thought it all looked comparatively simple, and wondered why our scientists on Earth had not stumbled upon this same procedure long ago. As I fathered this thought, without expressing it in words, my companion answered, "They have, to some extent. This is not very different from your tape and other kinds of recordings. The principle is the same, only we have carried it further. Instead of stopping with the gathering together of the many frequencies for sound reproduction alone, we are now able to translate them into picture form as well. You do this in a small way in the entertainment which you call TV. But in this, too, you are still bound by your limited knowledge."

During the time that he was explaining this to me, he had been intently watching the many screens. As he finished his explanations, he suggested that we go to the disk room to watch the return of these little messengers.

We had no more than reached the other room when the same two trap doors, looking much like large portholes in the wall of the ship, opened to receive each returning small disk. They settled into place as though quietly set down by some unseen hand.

I was given no time in which to react to the latest wonders now taking place, for Zuhl said quietly, "Keep watching! Another disk on each side is being sent out -- this time for a different purpose. We arc still in your atmosphere and when these have left, we shall return to the laboratory, where you will he shown how they operate."

As I watched, the trap doors adjoining the first two disks quickly closed behind them. Farther down the line two other doors opened, one on each side of the room. 'All the while, the women continued playing a nimble, silent scherzo above the instrument panels.

As the second pair of disks left the ship, we three returned to the large laboratory room. For the first time, I now noticed two other screens in operation. These were divided into sections. Zuhl explained, "These are showing the many atmospheric conditions." In one section I could watch the movement of air, while its speed and consistency were being registered by other instruments as the signals moved across the face of this screen. The electric charge or magnetic force of the atmosphere seemed to be moving in an opposite direction, and could be seen on another section of this screen, while its composition (a light or heavy load, as I understood) was measured and registered. On still a third section, many of the gases of which the atmosphere is composed were separated, and here I could see rapid changes of combinations constantly taking place. The different intensities of atmospheric pressure and many other conditions of which our scientists are totally unaware were remarkably interesting to watch. While this was being reproduced on the screens it was simultaneously registered by other instruments for permanent records and future study by the inhabitants of other worlds.

After what seemed only a few minutes the disks were attracted back into the carrier, and I was told that they contained within them samples of our atmosphere. These would be extracted and studied later.

"It was by means of disks like these," Zulu told me, "that we first became alerted to the abnormal condition building up on the fringe of your atmosphere -- a condition constantly increasing with every atomic or hydrogen bomb that is exploded on Earth. And since these instruments are in operation at all times, they tell us what we can expect as we move through space."

As we stood talking in the laboratory, my attention was drawn to a particular screen by the pilot. "You see there," he said, "visual images of the dust which you call 'space debris.' These are now being flashed back by two of the disks."

It was fascinating to watch the behavior of these tiny particles of matter on the screen. There was a constant swirling activity. Sometimes the fine matter would seem to condense into the semblance of a solid body, only to disappear and revert to practical invisibility. Occasionally, these formations became so rarefied and fine that they seemed almost to have been transmuted into pure gases. In a way, it reminded me of little white clouds suddenly forming in a clear sky, perhaps to grow larger, then as quickly to disappear into nothingness. This, at least, is the best analogy I can draw in describing the activity I witnessed on these screens.

Yet, with each formation of particle bodies, certain quantities of energy seemed actually to take visible, solid form, then immediately again be dissipated by what seemed an explosion or sudden disintegration, plainly visible on the screens. Other instruments recorded intensity and composition.

Sometimes these accretions formed with great intensity and the ensuing "explosion" was equally violent. At other times they were very mild and barely detectable.

But the cycle was ceaseless; whirling energy, solidification, disintegration; a perpetual motion of energy and fine matter ever seeking to combine or react with other particles in space. I use the term "energy" because I can think of no other word for what I was observing. It seemed to contain great power, and I noticed that when gathering into a sheet-like formation or cloudlike body, it appeared to disturb everything near it in space.

I believe that I actually witnessed the very force that pervades all space, from which planets, suns and galaxies are formed; the same force that is the supporter and sustainer of all activity and life throughout the Universe.

As this realization began to dawn upon me, I seemed unable to do more than half accept the tremendous implications. Zuhl, sensing my inner bewilderment, smiled affirmatively and said, "Yes. And this is the same power that propels our ships through space."

For a little while longer I watched the screens, full of wonder at what I was beholding. Then my companion drew my attention back to the disks. "These small Saucers are often seen moving through space, and sometimes low over Earth. At night they are luminous. They fly over Earth registering the various waves that emanate from the body of the planet -- waves which, like everything else, are in constant motion, with continual changes in wave length and intensity. Whenever possible these complex and highly sensitive little machines are returned to their parent craft, but sometimes, for one reason or another, the connection is broken and they go out of control or crash to the ground. In such cases emergency procedure is immediately brought into action. On each side of the mother ship, just below the disk-launching ports, is a magnetic ray projector. When a disk goes out of control, a ray is projected to disintegrate it. This accounts for some of the mysterious explosions that take place in your skies which cannot be accounted for by artillery, jet planes or electrical storms. On the other hand, if a disk goes out of control near the surface of the planet where an explosion might cause damage, it is allowed to descend to the ground where a milder charge is sent into it. Instead of an explosion, this causes the metal to disintegrate in slow stages. First it softens, then turns into a kind of jelly, then a liquid, and finally it enters a free state as gases, leaving not a wrack behind. This latter process is without danger to anyone or anything should the disk be touched while in process of disintegration. The only harm could come if, by chance, someone should see it fall and touch it at the moment the ray is applied."

When the Saturnian described the magnetic ray, I thought what a wonderful protective device it would be against anyone or anything attempting to attack their ships.

Receiving my thought, he replied, "Yes, it is entirely possible to use these machines against people, or any form whatever, including planets. But we have never done so, nor will we ever use them in that manner, for if we did, we would be no better than your people of Earth.

"Our protection, as has many times been demonstrated when pursued by your Earth planes, is our ability to escape faster than your eyes can perceive. Moreover, we can increase the frequency of the activated area of a ship to the point of producing invisibility. Except for our own precaution, your planes could fly blindly into our ship without seeing it. If we permitted you to come as close as that, when you hit, you would find our craft as solid as though functioning in a lower frequency. The impact would destroy you, yet do us no harm whatsoever.

"From what I have been told," I said, "I gather that occasionally something can go wrong with even your wonderful craft."

"Yes," he replied. "In such cases, if in outer space, we can abandon the ship if it is not salvageable. When this is necessary, the ship is disintegrated and returns to the original elements of space. Every large carrier is equipped with small emergency craft stocked with sufficient supplies and all necessary instruments with which to communicate to other ships in space, or even with a planet. However, if such an accident should take place near some planet, then we would crash just as your own planes do."

Instantly I asked him, "Then everybody on board is killed?"

"Yes," he replied, "but because of our understanding, death in your sense does not appall us. Each of us recognizes himself as the intelligence and not the body. Thus, through rebirth, we receive a new body.

"Also, because of our understanding, we can never deliberately destroy another body through which intelligence is expressing. However, if we should cause death unintentionally, through an accident, then we are not held responsible, for it was not of our own desire."

The instruments continued working as we stood talking. While I watched the screens flashing, I wondered if there were still more and different machines or instruments which I had not yet seen.

Replying to this unspoken thought, Zuhl answered, "Yes, there are many more in another large room between the disk room and the pilot's compartment which are in operation only while we are flying interplanetary."

During this visit to the laboratory and disk room, I had been totally unaware of the passing of time. I did not know whether we were standing still in Earth's atmosphere or moving rapidly through space since, although I had been watching the screens, I was unable to read them as the others were doing. But now the Saturnian pilot said, "We are not too far from your Moon."

To which remark I thrilled in excitement and wondered if we were going to land there.

"No," he said, "not this time. But we want you to see for yourself what you have been surmising about your Moon. The Moon has air, as you can see by our instruments, now that we are close enough to register it. Air is not naturally an obstruction to the viewing of another body, as we have sometimes heard it said on your Earth. And while, from your planet, you do not see dense clouds moving above the Moon, your scientists have on occasion observed what they call 'mild movement of air,' especially in pockets of these valleys which you call 'craters.' In reality, what they see are shadows of clouds moving.

The side of the Moon that you see from Earth has not much chance to show you its actual clouds, which are rarely heavy. While just beyond the rim of the Moon, over that section which might be called a temperate zone, you will notice by our instruments that there are heavier clouds forming, moving and disappearing, very much as they do above the Earth.

"The side of the Moon which you can see from your planet is quite comparable to your desert areas on Earth. It is hot, as your scientists correctly claim, but its temperature is not so extreme as they think. And while the side which you do not see is colder, neither is it as cold as they believe. it is strange how people of Earth accept statements from those they look up to as men of learning without questioning the limitations of that knowledge.

"There is a beautiful strip or section around the center of the Moon in which vegetation, trees and animals thrive, and in which people live in comfort. Even you of Earth could live on that part of the Moon, for the human body is the most adaptable machine in the Universe.

"Many times you Earthlings have accomplished what has been termed the 'impossible.' Nothing in the imagination of man is actually impossible of achievement. But to return to the Moon, any body in space, whether hot or cold, *must* have a kind of atmosphere, as you have named it, or gases that will permit this action to take place. Yet your scientists, while maintaining the absence of air around the Moon, do admit that there are both heat and cold on that body! The Moon does not have as much atmosphere as your Earth has, nor as our planet, because it is a far smaller body than either. Nonetheless, an atmosphere is present.

"Perhaps I can illustrate my point a little more clearly," the Saturnian continued. "You have on Earth a small island out in an ocean. As far as the eye can see there is no other land, yet men can live on this island as well as they did on the larger bodies which you call 'continents.' Bodies in space are like islands. Some are large and some are small, but all are surrounded and supported by one and the same power that gives them life.

"Many of your scientists have expressed the idea that the Moon is a dead body. If this were true and the Moon were dead, according to your meaning of that word, it long ago would have vanished from space through disintegration. No! It is very much alive and supports a life which includes people. We ourselves have a large laboratory just beyond the rim of the Moon, out of sight of Earth, in the temperate and cooler section of that body."

I asked him if the ship would go close enough so that I could see the surface of our satellite with my own physical eyes.

He smiled and said, "That will not be necessary. Come and look -- with this instrument we can bring the Moon up to within a short distance of where we are, so that you will be able to see it as clearly as if you were walking on it."

I asked him how far we now were from the Moon, and was told, "About forty thousand miles."

I hoped very much that we might circle the Moon, so that I could see for myself what was on the other side in that temperate zone he had mentioned. At the same time I realized that there might be things there which they did not care to have me see. And to this thought came a quick confirmation from the Saturnian pilot.

"We must test you with the information already given you before we reveal some things. We realize, perhaps better than you, the weaknesses of men, even of those who have a great desire to do right. We must be careful not to add to Earthly destruction."

As the instrument for viewing the Moon at close range was adjusted, I was amazed to see bow completely wrong we are in our ideas about this, our nearest neighbor. Many of the craters are actually large valleys, surrounded with rugged mountains, created by some past terrific upheaval within the body of the Moon.

I could see definite indications that, on the side which we see from Earth, at one time there must have been plenty of water. Zulu said, "There is still plenty on the other side, as well as much hidden deep within the mountains on this side." He then pointed out to me, up on the flanks of the mountains surrounding the craters, definite traces of ancient water lines.

True, some of the craters had been formed by meteorites hitting the Moon's surface, but in every such case, these craters showed definite funnel bottoms. And as I studied the magnified surface of the Moon upon the screen before us, I noticed deep ruts through the ground and in some of the imbedded rock, which could have been made in no other way than by a heavy run-off of water m times past. In some of these places there was still a very small growth of vegetation perceptible. Part of the surface looked fine and powdery, while other portions appeared to consist of larger particles similar to coarse sand or fine gravel. As I watched, a small animal ran across the area I was observing. I could see that it was four-legged and furry, but its speed prevented me from identifying it. Little of what I was seeing was strange to me, because for years I had been thinking and talking about it in much this way.

The Saturnian appeared aware of this, for he stated that it was partly for this reason they had decided to give me this close view now. He promised that, at some later date, they would show me the other side of our Moon. "This, too," he added, "will not be too different from the way you have imagined it."

As the promise was made to me, the screen showing the Moon went blank, although the other screens continued to operate.

Zuhl led me again toward the disk room, but before we reached it the ladies came out to meet us. The six men who had come down in the elevator with us rose from their seats as the Saturnian pilot suggested that we return to the lounge.

--()--

CHAPTER 10

ANOTHER MASTER

Once more in the beautiful and restful lounge, I noticed that the glasses on the large oval table had been refilled. A man whom I judged to be perhaps in his late thirties or early forties was awaiting our arrival. As we entered the room he rose from his chair. Without introductions of any kind, his greeting to me was as cordial as it was toward all the others, whom he must have known well. For my part, it seemed that here was one who was no stranger to me, and for whom I felt instantly the deepest affection and a kind of kinship. No doubt, at one time or another, my readers have had a similar experience. And his presence added immeasurably to the feeling of harmony and understanding among all of us gathered in the room.

With a slight gesture of his hand, he motioned us to seats around the table. A chair had been added, directly opposite mine, in which he took his seat. Again Firkon sat on one side of me and Zuhl on the other. At the invitation of the master, who now acted as host, each lifted his glass and sipped from it in silence. All were obviously waiting for him to speak. His dark brown eyes sparkled as with a deep joy of living, but I knew that they were capable of looking at my every thought. I knew, too, that whatever he might find, he would understand and not condemn.

He was a well-built man, firm of flesh. There were no gray strands in his black, well-trimmed hair, which was very thick and lay combed back in soft natural waves from a high forehead. The bony structure of his face was strikingly beautiful, giving the impression of having been endlessly refined by the spirit that dwelt therein.

His glance, full of a great kindness, traveled quickly from face to face. Then, in a voice that was soft and vibrant, he addressed me directly.

"We have been happy to show you a very small portion of our Father's Universe. We know of your interest in this subject, one that has absorbed most of the years of your life on Earth. Now, with your physical eyes you have seen registered on our instruments many things of which you have long been aware in consciousness. These experiences should give you confidence and greatly aid you in explaining the universal laws to those in your world.

"Never cease to point out to them, my son, that all are brothers and sisters regardless of where they have been born, or have chosen to live. Nationality or the color of one's skin are but incidental since the body is no more than a temporary dwelling. These change in the eternity of time. In the infinite progress of all life, each eventually will know all states.

"In the endless vastness of the Infinite are many forms. This you have seen on the two visits within our ships, out beyond the limits of your own atmosphere. These vary in size, from infinitely small dust particles, invisible to the human eye, to the largest planets and suns without number. All are bathed in the sea of One Power, supported by the One Life.

"On your world you have named the many forms which you have seen -- man, animal, plant, and so on. Names are but man's perceptions, while in the infinite sea names as you use them are meaningless. The Infinite Intelligence cannot name Itself, for It is all-complete. And all forms have been, and always shall be, dwelling within the Complete.

"Among the many forms, the one which you call 'man' professes to possess the only true intelligence upon your Earth. Yet this is not so. There is no manifestation upon your world or anywhere within the limitless Universe that does not express intelligence in some degree. For the Divine Creator of all forms is the expresser through Creation; it is His manifestation, a thought-expression of His intelligence.

"As a man, you are no more and no less than this. For the very life by which every form is supported, and the intelligence that expresses itself through it, is a Divine expression.

"Earth man, for the most part, not knowing this, finds much fault with many things outside his personal self, not realizing that each form expresses its purpose and renders the service for which it was made.

"There is no form that is capable of judging another, since all forms are but *servants* unto the One Supreme. None knows all that is to be known, since none knows all that is. This is known only to the All-Knower. But all forms, by serving willingly, grow in understanding of the source from which they receive their wisdom: the same life-force by which they exist.

"In the full conception, all manifestations of all forms are like beautiful flowers in a vast garden where many colors and many kinds bloom harmoniously together. Each blossom feels itself through the manifestation of another. The low looks up to the tall. The tall looks down to the low. The various colors are a delight to all. The manner of growth fills their interest and intensifies a desire for fulfillment. In observing the beauty unfold that lies dormant within, whether in a day or a century, design gradually becomes manifest -- in color, in a fragrance sweet to all others. Each glorifies itself by service rendered unto others; and in turn, receives from all others. All in that great field of beauty are the givers and the receivers, vessels through which flows a melody from the Highest.

"Thus some serve at the foot of the throne, while others serve above the throne and all around it. Each blends with every other, expressing only joy because privileged to serve. "It is likewise that the human expression which you know as man should have learned to live in the beginning of his dwelling upon your world. But in this lesson he failed. Had he not, your Earth would have been a garden of joy -- the garden of an everlasting desire to serve. But man, in his lack of understanding, has destroyed the harmony of his being on your Earth. He dwells in enmity with his neighbor, his mind divided in confusion. Peace he has never known; true beauty he has not seen. No matter how he prides himself on his material achievements, he lives still as a lost soul. "And who is this man that dwells in such darkness? He is the mortal] one who has failed to serve the Immortal One! It is he who speaks of 'The Path,' but seeks not the way to go. It is he who fears all things beyond the understanding of his fettered mind. lit is he who has denied the hunger of his spirit.

"And the fear which man has literally become stands firm in its guard against all life, against all things. For if this fear should move out of its own shadow, it would cease to be. This it is which holds man a prisoner until the end of his mortal side.

"Indeed, man dwells on Earth today desolate under the fear and dread of what he calls death -- the end of his mortal life -- alone in the wilderness of his personal darkness. Yet man himself has brought about the desolation which he so bitterly deplores, all because of service not rendered as it is naturally rendered by the humbler forms that surround him. Instead, man continues to destroy other life manifestations that he may survive. He has failed to realize the richness that these others could bestow upon him, would he allow them to serve as they were meant to serve.

"Alas, man's plot upon Earth is barren indeed. The seeds he sows with his small understanding yield bitter fruit. Still he remains fettered to his ignorance, repeating his errors through the centuries, still hoping to find that for which his heart longs, and for which his soul cries out.

"He is fearful of turning away lest that upon which he stands -- the Earthly foundation he has built for himself -- may be taken from him by another, and he will have nothing. So he keeps guard over that which is not eternal but, by the moment, is in process of change and decay, his eyes blind to what is happening. He has imprisoned within himself the light that could have guided him over the road of Eternal Oneness; a joy that all others who have gone that way have actually become. These are the servants, sons and daughters of the One Father, in all worlds. The Father, Creator of that beautiful field of the many forms, the many colors, the many shades, the many heights and the many depths -- the many delights that play and express, by day and by night, the one song of celestial harmony in which all may join."

As he spoke, pictures of his words passed vividly before me and again my understanding of man's plight upon Earth was quickened. As he ceased speaking, no one stirred. Nor did I wish to break the silence.

As the pictures ceased flowing through my mind, the master rose from his seat opposite and walked around the table toward me. All rose then and remained quietly standing.

The great teacher touched my hand lightly, and my whole being sang in humble gratitude for that which he had given to me. I gladly would have stayed in his presence forever, but I knew from previous experience that this was not to be.

"My son, do not be discouraged if you meet with ridicule and disbelief on your Earth. With the understanding we have given, you will know why it cannot be otherwise. Tell your brothers and sisters what you have learned. There are many with open hearts and minds, and these will grow in numbers.

"The Scout is waiting and our brothers will accompany you back to Earth. Now that we have been together in this way, you can the more easily at all times make contact from your mind to ours. Remember always that space is no barrier."

His words filled me with a contentment that allowed of no emptiness. Bidding me farewell, he turned and left the room. In a moment, Firkon and Zuhl motioned to me. I said good-by to my new friends, and when the lounge door slid silently open for us, we made our way across the elevator platform and into the waiting craft.

Slowly we descended, silently gliding down the rails, away from this gigantic laboratory carrier. As we glided Earthward, I glanced back at the large ship waiting there in space for the return of this little one. I wondered just how large it really was. ... .

Although my thought remained unspoken, Zuhl replied, "You might estimate it to be, in your figures, about three hundred feet in diameter and something like thirty-five hundred feet in length. These are not exact figures, but close enough."

It seemed but a matter of seconds before the door of the Scout opened and we were back on Earth. Farewells were said within the Scout, for the pilot did not come out with us.

The Martian and I walked to where we had left the car several hours earlier and set off on the journey to the hotel. I glanced back toward the Scout and saw it fast disappearing from sight, far up in our atmosphere.

As on the previous occasion, we were silent during the drive back to the hotel. I had much to think about and had no inclination to talk. I recall that the air held an early morning freshness and the first rays of the sun were just breaking through. So absorbed was I in remembering the master's words that I paid no attention to the scenery through which we passed.

When the car drew up in front of the hotel, Firkon touched my hand in the usual manner as he said, "We shall meet again."

I knew that we would and, although back on Earth in body, in consciousness I was both on Earth and with my friends of other worlds as they journeyed on through space. It was wonderful to know that we were not separated, that we never again could be separated! This night, a realization which had lain dormant within me throughout this present life's journey had suddenly blossomed into an awakening, even as the flowers in the garden which had been described to me by the wise one. The joy within my heart from this realization was as the melody of inanity, blended without separation or division. And I hoped and prayed that a way might be revealed whereby I could share Ibis realization with others upon the Earth.

I returned to my room in the hotel, but not to sleep. My experiences of the night had so strengthened and invigorated me that I felt like a new man, my mind awake and alert with thoughts more vivid and swift than ever before! My heart sang with joy, and my body was freshened as though from a long rest. There was much to be done this day, and tomorrow I must return to my home on the mountain; but from now on I would, to the best of my ability, live each moment as it came, complete in its fullness, serving the One Intelligence as man is in-tended to do, and for which purpose he was created.

--()--

CHAPTER 11

CONVERSATION IN A CAFE

About the first of September I began to get the feeling that soon I would again be seeing our friends from space. Often during the summer Iliad watched their ships moving through our atmosphere, but apparently the need for personal meetings had not arisen.

With each day that passed I felt a greater urgency to return again to the city. On September 8th, a friend who had been spending some time with us at Palomar Gardens invited me to drive to Los Angeles with her. I accepted, and at about four o'clock in the afternoon we arrived in the city. I registered at the usual hotel, accompanied the bellboy to my room, freshened up a bit and returned again to the lobby.

To my great surprise and pleasure, there-waiting for me, and smiling broadly, were Firkon and Ramu!

After greetings were exchanged, I asked if they were in a hurry. As if knowing my thoughts, Ramu replied, "Not in the least. We are here to answer any questions which you have in mind -- to the best of our ability," he added, smiling.

I suggested that we go to the little restaurant where we could eat arid talk without being disturbed. As we walked along, I said, "I suppose you are quite aware of the chief thing that is bothering me.

Firkon smiled and said, "Perhaps you are wondering whether the answers to those mental questions you shot into space this summer really got back to you without the wires crossed?"

"Exactly!" I exclaimed with a sigh of relief.

Due to the early hour, the restaurant was nearly empty. We sat down in a booth at the far end and ordered sandwiches and coffee. I explained to the waitress that we had dropped in more for the purpose of discussing a little business in a comfortable spot than to eat. She urged us cordially to make ourselves at home, served us quickly and left to resume her conversation with the cashier.

"What about that scoutmaster in Florida," I asked, "and the reports that some kind of flame had been directed at him from the Saucer?"

"Never!" Firkon replied emphatically. "We don't do things like that. What actually happened was that the man was frightened. Not wanting to reveal this by running away, he began hacking at the ship with his machete, hardly knowing what he was doing. Anyway, he came too close to the power that operates the Scout and got burned.

"To make it a little clearer," he went on, "you know that a rope has no fire in it, yet will cause a burn when pulled too quickly through the hands. In much the same way, the power emanating from the Scout passed over this man's body very rapidly, causing the body, acting with resistance, to be burned."

"You had a similar experience," Ramu reminded me, "on your first meeting with Orthon when your arm was caught by the power pulsating below the Scout. You were not actually burned, but you would have been had you lost your balance and fallen under the flange. Orthon saved you by pulling you back."

I then asked how much truth there was in the Brush Creek reportings.

"Those sightings were actual," Firkon replied, "although the craft and people are not part of our group. There have been many similar sightings and personal meetings with one or more individuals apart from yours; some before and some since your first contact. These have occurred in almost every nation in the world. Your experience, however, was the first reported in a way to reach great numbers of people.

Although such contacts have been taking place for years and records of them made which were never released, few men dare relate their experiences because of the incredulity of their fellow men."

He added very simply, "We do not enjoy the secrecy with which we have to make such meetings. We would far rather be welcome to come and go, and to visit with your people as we do with those of other worlds. But so long as our visits are not understood and are therefore made dangerous for us and for our ships, we will have to continue with the present caution."

I asked for information as to what had really taken place when Captain Mantell met his death.

Ramu explained, the sincerity of his feeling showing clearly. "That was an accident which we regretted deeply. The ship he was pursuing was a large one. Members of the crew had noticed Captain Mantell coming toward them and knew that his interest was sincere, not belligerent. They slowed down their craft and attempted to contact him through his instruments. They were fully aware of the power radiating from their ship and thought it would halt his approach without injury to him. But as he came closer, the wing of his plane cut through this power, allowing a suction to take place which pulled the entire plane into it, causing an immediate disintegration of both the plane and his body.

"This disintegration," Ramu further explained, "takes place through a magnetic radiation that separates the molecules which hold material together, completely changing their position. If his plane had bee-n round, or cigar-shaped, the accident would not have happened. His plane was not uniform in shape.

The wings protruded beyond the body of the ship, and it was a wing that was the cause of the accident. The fuselage would not have caused sufficient suction to pull the plane in, but once the wing was caught in the power, the remainder of the plane was sucked in so fast that it was reduced to small pieces of debris falling to the Earth, with some portions totally converted into dust particles.

"On the other hand," he continued, "we can come alongside our own ships and nothing of this kind would take place because we design our ships in a way which permits them to equalize any impact.

"The space craft's intent was merely to reduce speed and make an attempt to communicate with him. We had not realized that his plane could not touch our power and stand up under it. You will lose many, many men flying this kind of ship, and especially your jet planes, for they are in danger not only from the radius of our power, but they can enter natural magnetic currents that would twist and destroy them. There are too many points sticking out from the bodies of your planes, for once the power hits any one of them, the ship is doomed."

This completed my list of questions concerning the outstanding contacts that had been brought to my attention during the summer. "You have verified my impressions in each case," I told my companions.

"Then perhaps we can try to cover in advance some of the many questions that will be asked of you in the future," Firkon suggested. "As you have been told before, planets and systems are constantly in the process of being formed, or going through the process of disintegration. A system of planets is much like any other form -- a certain period of time is required to reach a peak of expression; then begins the process of decline and disintegration. Long before our system was even in the making, there were systems of planets without number on which were human beings such as you call mankind.

"Then, as today, there was interplanetary travel within systems and between systems. The main purpose for such travel was the same as ours is now -- to study the activities of space in all of its phases. So, when a new planet within a system of planets was found to be in the making, these were observed and studied closely by travelers from many worlds.

"When a new planet is found to have developed to the point where it is ready for human habitation -- and all planets reach that stage, sooner or later -- the travelers let this fact be known to the inhabitants of other worlds and of worlds in other systems. Volunteers are sought who desire to go forth and develop the new world. Then large ships take these volunteers, with all essential equipment on board, and move them to the new planet. Frequent additional trips are made to bring equipment and supplies to these pioneers, as needed. People are also carried back to their native planets for visits. In this way new channels of expression are opened and, simultaneously, a new world inhabited by mankind.

"The Earth was the slowest planet in our system to reach the stage where it was capable of maintaining human life. The first inhabitants of Earth were brought to it from the other planets. But it was not long before something unexpected took place in the atmosphere surrounding the Earth, and the transplanted people realized that within a few centuries living conditions on this globe would not be favorable. As a result, the first inhabitants of Earth, with a few exceptions, packed all of their belongings into space ships and left for other worlds. The few who chose to remain had permitted themselves to deteriorate amidst the lush beauty and abundance of this new world and sought nothing different. Gradually, they became content to live in natural caves and were eventually lost in the annals of time.

"On your Earth there is no record of these earliest inhabitants other than the mythology of one of your races in which the memory of this first civilization is preserved in what they call the god Triton, named after the original race of Triteria.

"Shortly after the departure of the space pioneers, many natural changes took place on the Earth's surface. Some lands were swallowed in the depths of the waters, while others rose. Then, once again, the world was ready for human habitation. But this time, because of the conditions still prevailing in the surrounding atmosphere, volunteers were not sought. Another condition that we had watched with interest in observing the formation and development of the Earth planet was the forming of only one moon as its companion. Under the natural law of conditions, this would result in an unbalanced state unless at some future time another moon was formed to complement the small companion of a growing world."

At this point Ramu was interrupted as the waitress came over to fill our cups with hot coffee. When she had left, Firkon said, "Man is a strange creature! *And* this is true wherever you find him throughout the vast Universe. Although the race of man as a whole prefers to live in peace and harmony with all creation, here and there a few will grow in personal ego and aggressiveness, and through greed will desire to assume power over other men. This can happen even on our worlds, despite the teaching which bids man live in accordance with the Divine laws."

"Yes," Ramu said, "and even though we know the evil toward which such attitudes lead, in conformity with the universal laws, we are not free to bind these brothers in any way. So, centuries ago, in a meeting among the teachers of wisdom on many planets, it was decided to ship such selfish ones to new planets capable of maintaining human life. In such cases, the planet of slowest development in many systems was selected for the exile of such culprits.

"So, for the reasons that I have just mentioned, the Earth in our system was chosen for the new home of these unruly ones from many planets inside and outside of our system. These exiles were what you on Earth call 'trouble-makers.' We could neither destroy nor confine them, since that is contrary to the universal laws. But as these people were all of the same arrogant nature, it was felt that, since none would yield to the other, they would eventually be forced to work out their own harmony. These are the true source of your original 'twelve tribes' on Earth.

"And so they were gathered in ships from the many planets and transported to Earth, without equipment or implements of any kind, such as volunteers are given. All had been well educated on their own worlds to know the soil, the minerals, the atmosphere and the many other things necessary for physical maintenance. Here on this new world they must use their knowledge and start with nothing more than nature herself provided. This was for the purpose of forcing them to work and draw upon their own talents, in the hope of bringing them back into the fold of all who do the will of the Creator.

"These are your Biblical 'fallen angels' -- the human ones who fell from a higher state of life and sowed the original seeds for the conditions which you now find existing in your world.

"For a long time after bringing these people to Earth, our people of many worlds visited them often, helping and guiding them as much as they would permit. But they were a haughty and defiant lot, and did not welcome the help we offered. Nevertheless, after the early clashes, for a long time they managed to live well enough with one another. At that time Earth was indeed a 'Garden of Eden,' since everything was plentiful and nature was lavish with her gifts of food and the necessities of life.

"In the joy of the new world, these newcomers began to dwell in peace and happiness with one another, and there was rejoicing on other planets. Then, as your Bible relates it, man ate of the fruit of the tree of 'knowledge of good and evil,' and divisions entered where before there had been none. Greed and possessiveness again became rampant amongst men and they turned one against the other.

"As time went on and the population increased, out of the original tribes arose self-exalted men who began to differentiate between the several races. Each demanded the rulership of the whole people, professing to have come from a planet further advanced than all the others, and by that right entitled to the ruling power. "We continued to visit these erring brothers, always with the hope of helping them to return to a brotherly relationship. As time went on, however, the self-appointed rulers became more and more powerful, and our efforts of less and less avail. The divisions continued and increased, finally resulting in the establishment of what you today call 'nations."

"The establishment of nations further separated brother from brother, and the whole of mankind lived no longer by the Divine law. "As a result of these divisions; many different ways of worship arose. But even then we continued to send others out in the hope of aiding our brothers on Earth. These men were those known as 'messiahs,' and their mission was to help their Earthly brothers to return to their original understanding. In each instance, a few followers would gather around these wise ones, but always they were destroyed by those whom they had come to serve. *"You* have wondered why Earth is the lowest planet in our system within a Universe of which we are all inhabitants. I have now told you.

"The people on all worlds which have been developed by men and women who volunteered for such service have gone steadily ahead. They have lived as the Infinite Creator intended that His children should live. They have grown and expanded in fulfilling the will of the Father. And each time that a group of volunteers leaves their own world to venture forth into a new one, after the Divine Hand has prepared it for human habitation, they are actually entering a new school of experience whereby they gain still greater understanding of a total Universe. Thus they fit themselves for continuous advancement into higher and higher states of expression and service.

"Labor such as you know on Earth has no part in their life, for as soon as the inhabitants of any planet work under the will of their Creator, the elements in turn begin to serve them.

"On Earth you have just the reverse. For, through self-exaltation and the perversion of natural law, man turns the elements against himself. Man warring against man is one of the most obvious examples of this, as he directs destructively the energies intended by his Creator for his welfare.

"And that is the primary difference between Earth's inhabitants and the peoples of other planets. Earth man has repeatedly attained certain peaks, only to enter into another stage of destruction which, through misuse of the elements, has destroyed all that he has accomplished.

"Here and there, an individual lifts himself above the majority on your world, since it is left to each man to speed up or slow down his own evolvement. Only when Earth men learn, by their own mistakes, that what they look upon as their strength is really weakness when pitted against the All-Divine Intelligence, and that their 'wisdom' but confusion against the All-Knowledge, will they be ready to return to the fold.

"Meanwhile, we keep ourselves ever alerted to receive the call for whatever help men of Earth may truly desire, for they are still our brothers."

"Do you never become discouraged," I asked, "in the face of such overwhelming odds?"

It was Firkon who said, "We know nothing of what you call discouragement. That is a negative word. Long ago we learned the power of faith and hope, and of never giving up. The goal lost yesterday can be won tomorrow. This does not mean that we believe ourselves developed to the fullest extent. Far from it. We have eternity yet to travel. But on our worlds, we no longer have sickness or poverty, as you know it; nor crime, as you know it. We recognize man as the highest representation of Deity, the consummation of all lesser forms. Should we with hurtful intent harm any form, we know that we would be forcing that form to turn from its natural purpose and do us harm. "You can see why the Creator has left us all to work out our own problems. When His laws are disobeyed, they witness against us. "You speak of Satan as though he were a separate en-my. But only by opposing the Divine principle can one create the inharmonious conditions which you have credited to Satan, and which you yourselves must correct. Then you will find that Satan becomes an angel of light, as your Scripture tells you. For all distortion must be corrected by the one who distorts."

As Firkon paused, Ramu's mouth curved in the slight, grave smile so characteristic, as he said, "The Sun rules not the Earth; nor does the Earth rule the Sun; nor do the stars rule each other. All are ruled by the Father. Here, from nature herself, does man begin to learn." For some reason, this called to mind a subject on which I had long pondered. "In regard to what we call death and rebirth," I asked, "should we be able to carry memories of the one life over into the next?" Ramu answered, "That is possible in varying conscious degrees. Eternal man forgets nothing. But the memory of things learned in a former body seldom manifests as more than an instinctive knowledge of, or gravitation toward, certain familiar things. In his conscious mind, Earth man has little understanding of why this is so. When such aptitudes manifest in lesser degree, you label them talents or gifts. When present to a very marked degree, and especially when present in childhood, you call such people prodigies.

"Your planet is functioning under what you might call a low frequency. As a result, the growth and development of form life -- and especially that of man -- is slow, requiring much time between birth and maturity. When men are born on Earth, they remain in a helpless infantile stage for a far longer period than on other planets. By the time they have reached manhood or womanhood, whatever memory may have come over them with them at birth is well buried under the welter of misconceptions with which, during all those early years, they have been filled. "Independent of natural law, man's reasoning powers are very limited. The newcomer is crammed with the traditions and conventions of past centuries, and the positive memory of previous experience is crowded out. Such genuine memory sometimes flashes up from what you call the subconscious into the conscious mind, through some channel suddenly opened. This can be caused by meeting for the first time a person whom you feel you have known, or by the sight of a place never before visited in this life, but with which you appear to have authentic associations and memories. "All such experiences are mystifying to most Earth people. Yet such memories are usually true memories and the explanation very simple.

"On other planets, we do not impose such blocks on the newborn child. On the contrary, everything is done to leave him free. We realize that each human expression is slightly different from every other, and that the individual background of experience serves as a foundation for the fulfilling of that particular destiny. "The frequency under which a planet functions can be established only by the inhabitants who dwell thereon. Due to the higher frequency of our planets, those born amongst us are not subject to the slow periods of development from infancy to maturity as on yours. With us, an average period of development from birth through adolescence is two years as compared with your eighteen or more.

"You on Earth use the term 'The Law of Transmigration' in a mistaken sense. What it really means is that when an individual on your Earth has risen above the ignorance of his brothers into a higher understanding of life, rebirth on another planet is permitted. He will come through with a vivid memory of his experience on Earth. Predominant will be his conception of the fundamental laws that govern all life.

Memories of his daily habits, his relationship with his family and associates, while still clear, will be secondary. He will realize that there are no missing links between the two stages of life, but a continuity of development uncluttered by the many names and divisions which confused him on Earth.

"Although the climb up from infancy to maturity requires so long a period on your Earth, age and deterioration come quickly. This is due to the old traditions and conventions which continue to be expressed in the individual. True knowledge, no matter how long ago it was acquired, is easily carried. But the burdens and woes of mankind repeated over and over again, remembered through centuries, weigh insupportably on the spirit of man. "As you have seen, we do not grow old in appearance or feeling. This is because we carry with us into each fresh day the bounty of lessons well learned, discarding all that has proven sterile. As we let the ever new and fresh express through us, we become that youthfulness.

"Just as the dream a sculptor has when he takes the clay into his hands will, when he has finished, decide the form the clay will express, so it is with the human body. Man is the sculptor of himself, working with materials supplied by his Creator. It is man's conception of himself within the Universe which will mold his body and imbue his features with beauty or with ugliness.

"In your world you picture the Deity as aged and yet eternal. This is a great contradiction, for eternity knows no age.

"Because of the endless activity going on within the depths and on the surface of your oceans, they survive through time. But a pond, wherein activity ceases, begins to show age by a mass of foreign matter that slowly dims its once clear waters. What you call stagnation has occurred.

"Bodily illness and disintegration derive from much the same process. Because you have not learned to live by natural law, personal stagnation sets in. Occasionally, even in your world, an individual can attain great age by your standards and still give the impression of youth. This is due to an ability to preserve the qualities of mental activity, interest and enthusiasm beyond the average.

I recalled a few such people I had known and nodded agreement. "You have indeed progressed far beyond us," I said. "Is it even to the point where your progress for-ward is never broken?"

This caused Firkon to smile. "Far from it! But when we make mistakes they serve as lessons for our future behavior rather than something to hide or try to justify. Moreover, when any new territory is being explored, whether physical or of the mind, we accept some error as inevitable. To you, what you call failure is shameful and often exposes individuals or groups to the ridicule and censure of others. This is a primary factor in binding Earth people to old ruts when, had they the courage, or their fellow men enough tolerance, they would try new ways. On our worlds, no man who sincerely tries is ever considered a failure, no matter what the results. That man has learned something. Through his very failure, he can make a great contribution to his fellow man. Courage and enterprise have led him to try a new path which, if proven wrong, need not again be trod by others. He alone has suffered willingly, and we, his brothers, commend him."

As Firkon stopped speaking and glanced at Ramu, I knew that this fruitful talk was at an end. Nothing needed to be said as we rose from the booth. We settled the bill and were again out on the street.

This time Firkon and Ramu did not accompany me back to the hotel. "I am very grateful," I said as we took leave of one another, the words sounding inadequate to my own ears.

I stood for a moment, watching them walk away, then turned in the opposite direction toward my hotel.

--()--

CHAPTER 12

AGAIN, THE GREAT MASTER

Not long after our conversation in the café, again following an impression, I found myself en route to Los Angeles. All during the drive to that city, I was filled with a kind of joyous anticipation that was like the remembered excitement I used to experience as a child just before Christmas.

The mental communications from my friends of other planets were becoming more and more definite as time went on. I knew now, for example, that this encounter would not be confined to a restaurant on the ground, but that they would again carry me up in one of their ships.

In this happy mood, the familiar beauty of the mountains through which we rode during the first part of the journey seemed enhanced to even greater majesty. And the valleys, surfaced with golden yellow in the natural state, or a shining green where cultivated, filled me with love for this Earth of ours. Surely, if mankind could learn only to look upon it with new eyes, there could be no room left for bitterness and strife

The time passed more quickly on this drive. I registered at the hotel, went briefly to my room, then returned to the lobby.

Although the clock above the desk showed the time to be only a little after 5 P.M., and I certainly was not hungry, I felt strongly impelled to go now for something to eat at the little restaurant, then return to wait for my friends. This I did and when, close to six o'clock I was again about to enter the hotel, Ramu stepped up to me.

I greeted him with delight and asked if I had kept him waiting.

"Not at all," he said, "I knew when to expect you!

The Pontiac was parked by the curb around the corner. As we got in, I asked about Firkon.

"He is unable to come with us this time," Ramu said, "and asked me to tell you that he is sorry to miss seeing you.

The mood of sustained happiness and anticipation remained with me all during the long drive out of Los Angeles and beyond. Occasionally, we exchanged a few words but for the most part there was little conversation.

Eventually we turned off the main highway and bumped along over a narrow road for perhaps half an hour. Searching the darkness for a first glimpse of the Scout, at last I saw a faint glow in the distance. As the outline became clearer, I knew from its size that it must be the Saturnian Scout, or a similar ship.

It was the same, and Zuhl was there to greet us. The journey to the hovering mother ship was quickly over. "Is this ... ?" I began, and Zuhl smiled and nodded, "The Saturnian ship you were on before? -- Yes." The landing procedure was accomplished exactly as on the previous visit. As Zulu led me in the direction of the large lounge, he paused a moment and said, "It was the master himself who asked that we bring you tonight. This visit is entirely that he may talk to you. If it was possible for my joy to mount higher, it did so on hearing this.

On entering, I was struck anew with the beauty of this room, and the harmony that filled it. All whom I had met before were present, and no strangers except for two beautiful women who resembled one another closely enough to be twins. I guessed, before introductions were made, that these were Saturnian women. On the right sleeves of their blouses, near the shoulder, were the same insignia I had seen on the shirts of the Saturnian men on the last visit. After my friends had welcomed me, I exchanged greetings with the two lovely strangers. There were differences both in their persons and garments from those of the other women. Since they remained standing close to me, I had an opportunity to check these in detail. Both women had very dark brown hair and eyes, and thick curling lashes. The complexions were of an almost startling whiteness with a rose cast in the cheeks; the lips were full and red. Both appeared to have a greater vivacity of manner than the other women. I believe, however, that this had nothing to do with the fact that they were Saturnians, but was rather a characteristic of their own personalities.

They wore light-blue blouses with long, full sleeves drawn in tightly at the wrists. These blouses were more like short jackets and were finished at the neck with a narrow rolled collar. The skirts were of the same color and material. The latter appeared very light in texture and of a quite different weave from any I had seen. The full skirts had wide waistbands and were ankle length, like those of the other women. They wore fawn-colored sandals on their small feet.

I did not see the master and presumed that the reason all remained standing was in expectation of his entrance.

"There is quite a bit of activity on the part of your air force tonight," Ramu told me, "and the ship is now rising. We shall probably remain hovering at about ninety thousand feet from your Earth."

Needless to say, I did not feel, nor had I felt, any movement whatsoever.

At this point the master entered and all turned toward him.

As his eyes met mine, he smiled and walked on to where a table was surrounded by low chairs with arms, covered with attractively upholstered material of an appearance something like dull silk.

Ramu led me over and the master indicated that I take the place on his right. One of the Saturnian ladies sat on my other side and while the people were settling into their seats, I seized the opportunity to ask if she could explain the meaning of the insignia. She obligingly twisted around so that I could examine the one on her right shoulder and said, "It denotes that Saturn is the Tribunal of this system." Although I did not know exactly what she meant by "tribunal," she did not explain further. The design consisted of a sphere encircled by a ring (much as the ringed planet appears through our telescopes), and inside the sphere was a balanced pair of scales.

Thanking her, I settled back into my chair and found it difficult to believe that anything could be so comfortable. Not even our air cushions yield to and yet support the body as did that chair. The master began to speak. "My son, if some of what you will hear tonight seems repetitious, it is because the things of which I shall speak are important to your understanding, and perhaps a fuller explanation will help you to retain them."

I was glad to hear him say this, since, even with the telepathic help which had been promised me, I still worried for fear I might not remember it all.

"A great fallacy which has grown on the people of Earth," the master said, "is the custom of dividing into many parts that which should never be divided. You have multiple divisions in forms and teachings, many firm likes and dislikes, all of which serve only to add to the state of confusion on your planet.

"We of other worlds have no such divisions but realize the relationship and the interdependence of all things. I know that you have felt deeply the power and radiance of our conception of Deity there on the wall before you. By keeping always this image visual before our eyes, and remembered in our hearts, we never forget that within Him all forms have their being.

"He is the giver of what you call life' unto men. He is also the giver of life through us to our creations in which He is the instructor of what is to be created. He it is who knows how the minerals and the elements are to be combined -- not only to serve us, but the Universe as well, ever better as they are brought up through the experiences of one form, to be fitted for a higher form. We on Venus, and on other planets in varying degrees of evolvement, recognize the minerals and elements as the essence of ever-active Divine expression, with a steady newness. And therefore monotony, as you know it on Earth, can never be.

"So, as the creation of a Divine Creator of the total Universe is respected by us, so also is the creation of man who guides the elements in different channels of service likewise respected and honored. In turn, the elements become desirous to serve better each day that they, too, may rise to a higher standard of service . . . a service which shall never cease, for it is eternal.

"As an example, that you may understand this more clearly, the bit of iron which you find among the minerals of your Earth serves you in one particular channel. Yet by impregnating this iron with a force which you call 'electricity' the iron changes from a previous service to another type of service called 'magnetic.' Therefore it has been endowed with a power of attraction which it did not have before. This is what we mean by elements or minerals evolving for a better service. For first it was merely the mineral iron; then it reached a higher state of service where it was able to attract, which in the original state it could not do. And so, on and on, this iron can evolve toward higher and higher service rendered unto its Creator.

"So you see what is meant when I speak of the minerals and the other elements serving man. By doing this, they themselves are endowed with certain powers of comprehension through serving the All-inclusive Intelligence. This law, I believe, is known to you on Earth as the Law of Transmutation, or the Law of Evolution.

"A human body like yours and mine is composed of elements as well as minerals. And you can prove that these elements and minerals which compose your body do obey the impressions placed upon them. For if the impressions are of a joyous nature, the being called 'man' is joyful. But if of an angry state, then the body expresses that, proving that the minerals and the elements within it are constantly serving the Intelligence. Without it they cannot rise to a higher state of expression.

"You men of Earth continually invite disaster by creating combinations which are opposing each other rather than working together. You have made of yourselves something other than your Divine origin. You have added many false concepts to your being instead of remaining natural; like a beautiful woman who is exalted in beauty, yet adds many trinkets that finally exalt themselves above her beauty. "You have done the same by adding that which had no true life or intelligence. Let me point out to you something inherent in the being of man by which we live on the planet Venus, while you do not, though these principles apply to yours as well as other worlds.

"You claim that you are a being made up of five senses, and list others to be added -- the sixth, seventh, and so on. You seek to develop these arbitrarily conceived senses instead of understanding and developing those which do exist. In professing that there are powers of clairvoyance, clairaudience, mental telepathy, or extra-sensory perceptions, you thereby divide one total phase of expression into at least four separate classifications. And, as a result, your true identities have become muddled and lost.

"Let me elucidate this a little. In the first place, you are a product by mineral and elements of what you call nature. In the second place, as an intelligent expression of that form, you are a product of your Divine Creator. The mineral and elemental part of your being has been endowed with *four* avenues, or senses, through which it expresses in what you call a physical manifestation. Intelligence or divinity expresses through every cell of the entire form which you have labeled physical.

"The four senses to which I have just referred are sight, hearing, taste and smell. Observe that I did not

mention the sense you on Earth speak of as 'touch.' Because touch is the *intelligence* that precedes all others.

"Let me explain it this way. No one in any world can build a form like yours, or cause it to live as do you. This can be done only by the Creator of the Universe. Therefore, you must admit that when conception of a form takes place within a form, that mother-to-be knows not what is to be done for the perfect construction of another body. Yet the conception grows toward a complete manifestation, until finally it is born into what you call the physical world.

"When it is born, this form complete has eyes, ears, mouth and nose. The eyes see, and the ears hear sounds for the first time; the nose smells and the palate tastes for the first time. These were all created as parts of the body. As the body witnesses the physical world for the first time, so do these four avenues of expression, for they are of the body. Yet the mother of this form knew not how it was built.

"But the sense of *touch,* which I omitted from the group of senses, did know. For remember, while the little one was still in the building process within the mother's body, if a pressure was put onto the mother's body, the body within was also alerted to that pressure. And notice the separation between the two, for when the body to be born was ready to make a change within the mother, the mother neither controlled nor instructed this action, which does separate, in this case, the sensation into two distinct reactions -- the mother's and the child's. This proves that each operates in the field of sensation or feeling independent of the other. Yet they arc a body within a body. Also proving that this thing called 'touch' or 'feeling' is acting in the field of intelligence, knowing what to do and when to do it. It seems to be the 'knower.'

"When we take this into consideration for the purpose of analyzing, the sense of touch is recognized as a cardinal one, or in reality the soul of the body -- part of the all-inclusive intelligence. For it is a feeling -- and feeling, as you know it, is a state of alertness, or conscious consciousness as we know it.

"Now, when this consciousness leaves the body of minerals and earth known as *man,* the eyes, the ears, the taste and the smell no longer function. For when the body becomes unconscious it does not recognize anything like a touch. In other words, you could beat that body and it would not have the sensation which is called feeling or of being touched.

"On the other hand, if one loses the eyes, loses the hearing, the taste and the smell, but retains the sense of touch, which is consciousness, one is more or less alive and intelligently operating. And when the body is then struck with something, it feels that touch or hurt, where it did not in the previous state.

"Thus it is easy to see that the real intelligence of the body called 'man' is that which has been so misused and mislabeled, the sense known to you as touch, which is the soul or the life of that body. The human *body -- and* the same is true of all other forms -- is actually constructed for services that its minerals and elements will render through the *four* major physical avenues of expression. While the fifth, *touch,* is a universal one which gives sensation to the other four. Once this touch sense leaves the other four have no power of sensation or operation.

"When man realizes this fact, he then finds himself as the real behind the mask. And when this is done, the limited prison in which he has lived for so long dissolves, and he becomes a dweller of the Universe. As such, he sees the law in operation in every form, regardless of what that form may be, and including the planet itself upon which he is living. Then does man *know* himself! And by so doing, he knows all things. Also he knows his. Creator as he has never known Him before, which is the Universal or Divine Intelligence.

"It is through this recognition or understanding that mineral man rises to a condition of unity with the Father, wherein the Father and the Son become one. Once the man of Earth learns this and realizes it, not knowing it with his mind alone, but by living it as we have done, he shall have the same joy in life as we have on other planets.

"As your Bible says, the prodigal son has thus returned home by giving up his physical mineral vanities and making these serve him for the service of his Father, rather than he serving them.

"Of course, my son, you know this law and have been trying to live as well as teach it for years. It is neither new to you nor is it any original teaching of yours. It is a universal law which all men must know and live if they hope to enjoy their Divine birthright as sons of the Father. "You must impress, as best you can, understanding in the minds of your brothers on Earth that knowledge of themselves is the first requisite. And the first questions:

"Who am I? Through what avenues can I express in order to return to the oneness from which I have fallen?"

"Remind them that Man has nothing to add. He has only to express that which already is his. But he must learn to understand what it is he has, and *live* this understanding. For it is the living that is important. Once this is accomplished, the Earthly man's woes will soon vanish. For then these elements which are used in making up the four senses of sight, hearing, taste and smell will begin to evolve to where they will become more .sensitive instruments, not only to serve in what you call the physical world, but also in service of the universal.

"Another fact which Earth men must realize is that 'universal' includes the physical within itself, not outside it. For everything which takes place within the Universe is also within the Divine or Supreme Intelligence -- not outside it.

That is why we are as much concerned with your world and your life as we are with our own, for we are all in the same kingdom of the Supreme Intelligence. "We have learned and lived this for all these hundreds and thousands of years. Because of this understanding, we cannot injure with a motive of injuring as you do on Earth. For we know that we would have to live with whatever we distorted, since all is within the household.

"Once the mind of physical man rises to this degree of understanding, it does not see anything as ugly or unpleasant, but sees all in the process of going toward the holiness of beauty and exaltation. "As Earth men consider this law, they will see and understand how all is working from the low to the high, which is the universal purpose; and not from the high to the low. Yet the power expresses from the high even unto the low that the low may have the strength to rise unto the high. There is eternal blending, but never division. Knowing this law, the inhabitants of our planets have used it for their development and through its use have grown to a recognition of everlasting life and the role of all therein."

The thought of overpopulation flashed through my mind as this is so often a topic of concern for nations on Earth. Without the slightest interruption, this man of great wisdom answered my thought.

"No, my son. We are not overpopulated and such a condition never threatens us, as it does your people of Earth. For we do not replenish without thought or planning as do you. There is a natural law of balance by which we abide. Besides, those who have attained much knowledge on one planet may, if they choose, seek rebirth on another. Toward this end they have two choices. They may make this change through the channel of birth, or be taken direct by a ship, still in the same body. This has happened many times, even on Earth. The vast majority have advanced from the Earth toward another planet through rebirth. Others, though few, have been taken direct as your Bible tells you.

"Death takes place upon other planets the same as on Earth. But we do not call it death, and we do not mourn for those who have left, as you on Earth do. We know this leaving means only a change from one condition or place to another. We realize that it is no more than a moving out of one house and into another.

"We cannot take our houses with us when we go from one place to another. Neither can we take a body, which is the house, from one world to another in death. The material of your Earthly bodies belongs to Earth, and must remain there to maintain your world. But when you move from Earth to another planet, that world will lend you of its materials to build a house according to the needs and conditions that exist there.

"Earth man's concept of the Universe is very small. He cannot conceive of a Universe without limits. Yet he uses the word eternity. Eternity, according to man's own definition, denotes no beginning and no ending. Then how vast is the Universe? As vast as eternity.

"So man is not a temporary manifestation. He is an *eternal* manifestation. And those of us who have learned this truth are living in a constant present, for it is always the present.

"We of Venus dress much as you do, and we do many things in a similar way. There is no great difference between our form and yours, or in the garments for that form. The great difference lies in our understanding of who we are.

"Since we have learned that life is all-inclusive and that we *are* that life, we know that we can hurt nothing without hurting ourselves. And life, to be life eternally, must remain in a prime state of its being, and to express this, must be ever new.

"Therefore, as I have said, monotony is never experienced by us. Each moment that passes is a joyous one.

And it matters not what work we have to do. If what you call labor needs to be done, we do it with full joy and love in our being. And on our planet, each day brings its quota of things to be done, exactly as on yours. Every man and every form is respected alike for the services they render. None are judged as to shortcomings. It makes no difference as to the kind of service undertaken, be it what you call menial or not. All services are equally acknowledged. "People on Earth have been given this law, for it was brought there by those who knew of it and who at one time practiced it on other planets. It was expressed in the building of Solomon's temple. The hiring of labor in the vineyard where all alike were paid a penny at the end of the day, as recounted by Jesus, your Messiah, was an acknowledgment of the equal honor in serving." As the great master paused and passed his hand lightly over his brow, I realized that I had been listening with such intentness that I had not stirred. Moving my body to a different position, I waited for him to resume speaking.

"Although the air on all planets differs slightly, contrary to the present beliefs of your scientists, Earth man could go anywhere in the Universe without discomfort. Indeed, this will be his natural heritage once he attains an understanding of himself and realizes the great adaptability of his form."

Again he paused and bowed his head slightly as though in meditation before he continued. "We have developed to a degree of conscious perception which does not permit us to sit amongst any group of people without the thought of blessing. For their very presence before us *is* a blessing because we do not see them merely as people, but as the Divine Intelligence in a living state through a form known as human. Our awareness is the same toward every form outside the human.

"We see the Divine Consciousness expressing Itself through the growth of any and all forms, from the smallest to the largest. We have learned that nothing, no form whatever, can be what it is without life passing through it, or supporting it. And the life we recognize is the Divine Supreme Intelligence.

"Never a moment passes, even in sleep, that we are not aware of this Divine Presence.

"This is the true purpose of the form 'man' ... that for which he was created. For, while all other forms give expression in their particular field of service, his is the evolved form of mineral and elements capable of expressing the highest state of Divine Intelligence.

"We are not on guard against one another, nor do we covet anything belonging to others. For we are all equal participants of the goods of our planets."

I understood clearly all that this great teacher of other worlds was saying, but a question entered my mind. I wondered how they viewed killing for food, if they did kill, or even consuming fruit and vegetables, since these too were living in their own form of expression. And as always, the answer came without my speaking.

"There is nothing illogical in this, my son. When you eat a lettuce leaf, it becomes a part of you, does it not? As a result, from then on it begins to experience things with you. So what you have actually done is to transmute one form into your own form. Had this not been the case, the lettuce leaf would have matured, then gone to seed in order to replenish its own kind again, and that would have been its total experience. But by serving you, it has been elevated to a higher service through you.

"Motive also enters into this principle. If your motive is to destroy or injure or exploit, then it is wrong. But if your motive embraces the service you can render another form by bringing it up to your standard, through you, then it is right. For you are really transmuting a mineral from one state to another that it may be of still greater service. In doing this, you are acting according to the law of growth or development, ofttimes called 'evolution' in your world. This is the law of your Creator.

"The people of your world make much of form -- disintegration -- not realizing the law of elevation, because they have begun to think that the form is all there is. But the form is only a channel through which life, or intelligence, expresses. All-Inclusive Intelligence cannot express through a lettuce leaf. So the lettuce leaf must be transmuted by gradual stages into a higher form through which to express greater service. That is the way it is rewarded.

"When this law is fully accepted and *lived* by your Earth men as it has been accepted and lived by inhabitants of other planets and systems, the atmospheric conditions of Earth will be sweetened. For every form will then give off joyous radiations from itself that will permeate the air within which mankind lives.

"You have wanted to know by what method we have evolved to the state in which we are now living. These are the fundamental laws by which we live, and by which Earth men can also evolve, if they choose to accept and live them.

"When men of Earth have learned that they are not the body or the house, but merely the *occupant* of the body or the house, they can build homes anywhere they will, for they too will become masters of elements in-stead of being mastered by them.

"While you of Earth have come into a knowledge of governing certain elements to certain points, misuse of your knowledge is widespread, and the elements are turning to destroy you, as many other civilizations on your Earth have been destroyed in the past.

"This is the stage in which we find Earth men today. We can but continue trying to help wherever opportunity presents itself, but it is difficult to reach in sufficient numbers minds so little developed as those of Earthly men.

The master was silent for a moment. Then he said, "This is not the first time you have been brought into our ships, nor will it be the last. You may rest assured that we of other worlds from time to time will bring you truth that you may pass it on to your fellow men of Earth. We will tell you of the physical life of other worlds, as well as what you call spiritual or religious truths, although we do not make that kind of division. There is but *one* life. That life is all-inclusive, and until men of Earth realize that they cannot serve or live two lives, but only one, they will be constantly opposing one another. That is one major truth that *must* be learned by all Earth men before life on your world can match life on other planets

"And now, my son, it is time for your return to Earth. What you have learned can be of great value to the people of your planet. Speak to them by word of mouth and by written word. Do not fear lest you forget any of what you have been told. For as you speak or write, with the first thought a continuous flow of memory will come to you.

In this beautiful ship of another world there was peace. The lesson of the night had been deep in understanding and meaning. Somehow, I knew that all had heard this same lesson, perhaps many times throughout their lives. But it seemed to be one that they loved, as if in the telling a new something opened within each listener and he grew larger in his own understanding. Again I wished I need not return to Earth, but that I might remain with these gracious friends and journey with them to other worlds. But the wise one said, "Son, there is much yet to be done on your Earth. The people are hungry and must be fed. You will return and share with them this food of the spirit that they may not perish in the darkness of ignorance that has prevailed upon your Earth throughout so many generations."

--()--

On the journey back I seemed still to hear the master's words falling with gentle insistence against my consciousness in the silence that remained unbroken by either Ramu, Zulu, or myself.

It was the same during the drive back to the city. I vaguely remembered taking leave of the pilot of the Scout, but I do not think any words were exchanged.

When Ramu stopped at the entrance of the hotel, I slowly stepped out onto the sidewalk. Then I turned, dimly aware of something I wanted to say. Although Ramu probably knew what it was before I myself, he waited quietly, understanding in his eyes and the grave smile on his lips.

Then, suddenly, it came to me. "The mental message I received this time," I said, "it seemed so much clearer ... I seemed to know more certainly when I left for Los Angeles what was going to happen. Did the master himself contact me mentally this time?"

"Yes," Ramu said, "he did. And that is largely responsible for the difference, although your own ability to receive is growing."

"But the -- the exaltation of spirit I felt," I went on, stumbling in an effort to express it. "I am sure that that must have come to me through the master."

"Yes," Ramu said again, "he is one of the most evolved beings still functioning within our system. Just to be in his presence is to grow in love and understanding. We are all fortunate."

We said our farewells and I went into the hotel.

As always after such meetings, I had no desire to sleep. This time I did not even look to see what time it was. I know that I stood a long while at the window, looking up, not down. I had the strange feeling of separation within myself that I had experienced before, only this time there was no sadness in it. I believe I may have spoken my thoughts aloud. "It is one. it is all one. There and here and everywhere. There is no separation. ...

--()--

CHAPTER 13

DAYS AT PALOMAR TERRACES

During the next few months, I had several more contacts, both in the ships and with people from other planets who are working anonymously amongst us.

Palomar Gardens had been sold and we moved a few hundred feet up our mountain. *Flying Saucers Have Landed* was released in England in September, 1953, and the American edition followed in October.

There was much to be done in opening up this new territory. Not only was it grown thick with live oak trees, but the land was filled with boulders. We often spoke wistfully of the knowledge known on Earth ages ago which enabled men to lift and move great slabs of stone as though they were feathers. The Egyptians who built the pyramids knew the secret, as did those who moved into place the great ancient statues found on Easter Island. But we were obliged to depend on snorting bulldozers to break a road up through our land and nose out the rocks.

Our little group passed many stimulating evening hours planning the simple buildings we would have liked to put up here, not just to take care of ourselves but also to accommodate the ever-increasing number of people who were coming up to see me. We had expected that the purchasers of Palomar Gardens would continue to operate it as a restaurant and modest guest house since there were no such accommodations within many miles from here. But, for some reason, they decided to close it. So, although we have no servants, we felt that we must give our visitors meals as a courtesy in view of the effort many of them made in planning time to come up for a visit.

We managed to build a kitchen unit convenient to level terrace we cut in the flank of our mountain. The terrace turned out to be a colossal job, but with the help of several muscular young men who gave their time, it was finally accomplished. Our efforts were well rewarded. A portion of the terrace is shaded by magnificent live oaks and we can look out to the tops of mountains, lifting one behind the other in soft pastels until the last all but blends into the sky. We equipped this spot with outdoor chairs, benches and picnic style tables and bought a small charcoal grill.

At first we all lived as best we could in two old cabins belonging to friends on a strip of land just next to ours. We used the kitchen unit, also serving as an office and a bedroom for one of us, as a meeting place when weather drove us indoors. As yet, we had neither running water nor electricity. A pure stream flowed underground down the side of our mountain. We piped this to the surface and made a little pool with an outlet so that the water was always fresh. This we carried up in buckets.

We knew that, in spite of our dreams and the need for such things, we could not just go ahead and have these buildings constructed until we had the money to pay for them. So, although our living would no doubt appear uncomfortably primitive to most people, and the labor hard, we were happy with what we did have, and every small contributing comfort to ease the daily chores that we could add from time to time meant more than if it had come easily.

It was a wonderful day when we knew that we could now put up a small building which would contain one fair-sized room where I could talk with my visitors in inclement weather, and a smaller room for a proper office.

We knew of a contractor in a small city about twenty-five miles distant who was honest and dependable, and we got in touch with him. The kitchen unit had been built entirely by ourselves and our good friends, some of whom had been my pupils in the instruction of universal law for many years. That first small unit will always mean a great deal to me because of the friendship and loyalty that made its achievement possible.

Now we could have a real contractor! He proved to be a very fine man and became interested in my work. The little cottage was quickly completed. We had enough money left to furnish it in attractive comfort. And here were two small lavatories with a shower between! Although we had no electricity until just a few weeks since the time of this writing, the water ran through the pipes, and what matter if it were cold -- and a mere trickle! The long wait for the electricity which now gives us heat and has made our candles and kerosene lamps obsolete was just one more delight, and worth waiting for.

While we were working our way toward our present comfort, we managed to support quite a bit of animal life in the style to which it was accustomed. These included two dogs and six cats, not to mention frequent well-conducted visits from their fellow creature, the skunk. These much maligned animals are disposed to be social and amiable when not antagonized, and they know friends when they see them. They drink milk from the cats' bowls and share meat with the dogs, seldom under protest from any animal. Occasionally, when one of the dogs decides to make an issue of it and rushes the interloper, yapping loudly, Mr. Skunk merely retires up the mountain side with grace and some speed, the upraised tail proving nothing at all.

Between lecture engagements which took me into the Middle West, New York and Canada, I worked on the premises in every capacity for which I was fitted, stopping only to talk to my friends and the many strangers who came to see me. Although I had lecture engagements scheduled for the East Coast, and in England, while in Canada I became very fatigued and lost my voice. The lectures were very close together and I seem unable to learn how I can save my strength when discussing the subjects closest to my heart. In addition to the formal lectures, many of my listeners naturally wanted to ask questions later. Somehow, I could not heed what I knew to be good advice in respect to leaving the lecture hail before these good people could get at me! As a result, I *couldn't* talk any more, and my doctor ordered cancellation of both the Eastern and the English lecture engagements, and a complete rest for at least six months.

This edict was a great disappointment to me for obvious reasons, but one to which I was forced to bow. Soon after my return to the mountains I love, I regained my voice and at least insisted on using it when visitors arrived.

I fear I must be a very troublesome proposition to those who try to make me behave with what they call some sense." Probably I simply have none. In any case, whatever I may spend of myself in giving as I can to those who have sought me out, I know that I receive far more in many ways.

In June of 1954, Desmond Leslie, whom I would have met for the first time in New York had I been able to carry out my program, came to Palomar instead. This was a great joy. Endowed with a very interesting mind and a delightful sense of humor, he added much to our little group here, not only in that he shared our common interests but also entered into the nonsense which often overtook us when relaxation from serious subjects was indicated.

Although he had expected to stay only a month or so, Desmond remained with us until late in August. I look forward to seeing him again in his country sometime in 1955 when I go over to fulfill the postponed lecture tour.

Altogether, what with the further meetings with my friends from other worlds, the increasing list of good friends on this world of many types and kinds, the good healthy outdoor work and putting together the material for this book, my days were very full and happy. Occasionally, I even rested when my friends began to look at me in a certain unpleasant manner!

We soon discovered that the purpose of the new cottage was going to have to be extended. So, just before Desmond's arrival, in order to provide a bedroom, we put a partition up in the center of the large room which we had planned as a forum and informal lecture hail. As it was, one of us was still sleeping in the old cabin -- and another still had a bed in the kitchen unit. So now, the new arrangements provided us with half a lecture room, in which I sleep, one proper bedroom and an office complete with a cot. We felt really set up when, shortly after, we transformed a pup tent into a comfortable sleeping place by raising it off the ground on a plywood base and running screen around the upper half. Thus, we got the bed Out of the kitchen!

I am still engaged in piping water in and out of tanks and round about the grounds (with some able *women* assistants!) and feel very proud of the results. The former trickle in wash bowls and shower is now a veritable torrent, and we have made a real little pool under a live oak tree and planted flowers around its rock border. Just this morning we took a cement cupid and a crane out from under the house and placed them in the pool. They look very pleased.

We work hard, but we are happy. The mountains are always there before our eyes, never monotonous in the beauty that changes with dawn, the full sunlight and the setting sun. They are lovely at dusk, whether touched with moonlight or dark against a sky full of stars.

And often we see the Saucers flashing overhead. In fact, in recent weeks the space ships have been seen by many in neighboring towns and cities. We are content to know that they are there above us, and in the skies of all our Earth. We hope that in the not too far distant future all peoples in our world may see and know them for what they are; and we hope that many of those whose words would convince, who do know now and have kept silence, will speak out in the interest of all mankind.

--()--

CHAPTER 14

THE BANQUET AND A FAREWELL

The latest contact occurred on August 23, 1954. Desmond Leslie was in Los Angeles at the time for the purpose of fulfilling a lecture engagement. He knew that I was about to have this contact and was most anxious to be taken with me. While I too hoped for this, the Brothers, for reasons which they did not give, were not able to grant the request. As I look back, I think it was because the nature of some of the things which were shown and explained to me this time were not designed for one without previous contacts. My friends Firkon and Ramu met me as usual. En route to the Scout, Firkon said, "I must tell you that tonight's meeting will be a farewell for you and for us. After we bring you back to your hotel tonight, we return to the Scout, and then on out to the carrier which will take us back to our home planets. Our mission on Earth is fulfilled."

A great sadness surged up in me.

Ramu said quickly, "But you are losing us only in bodily form. Don't forget that we can still communicate mentally, wherever we are. I took what comfort I could from this thought, but at the moment it seemed little enough. Then Firkon said, his voice full of comprehension, "You are our friend, and all the space that may stretch between us can never change that." I felt ashamed of my emotion. Although I could not entirely banish it, I did manage to rise above it to some extent. I found myself wondering if some other "contact" man, or men, living temporarily on our Earth, might possibly be assigned to meeting me in future. But to this unspoken question, neither vouchsafed an answer. I was left with the feeling that this might indeed be farewell, at least for some time to come, not only to the two friends between whom I now sat as we rode along, but to any further excursions into space.

This emotion, as I think can be imagined, lent to all the new and wonderful things I was to see this night a poignancy which quickened my deep appreciation. This, added to the gratitude for what had already been granted, produced a fullness in my heart that I could never put into words.

Inasmuch as I have already described in detail a journey in this same Scout, I shall state only that I found Orthon awaiting us with the little ship hovering slightly above the ground, ready for an immediate take-off. On this trip we did not even sit down. I divided my attention between watching the changing graphs and Orthon at the control panels. As we entered the Venusian carrier, this time I was entirely free of any dropping sensation in the pit of my stomach. We reached the platform and stopped again, as on our first trip. The same man was there to attach the clamp over the Scout for its recharge, but this time he followed us down the steps and into the lounge.

Immediately on entering, I was struck by a general air of festivity. There were a great many people present whom I had never seen before. I was delighted when I saw Ilmuth and Kalna coming forward to greet me warmly. "Did anyone tell you about the surprise we have for you tonight?" Kalna asked, and without waiting for a reply continued enthusiastically, "A certain promise made to you will be fulfilled!"

While Kalna was speaking, Ilmuth had given me a goblet of the delicious fruit juice. I noticed that both girls were dressed in pilot uniforms and I felt sure this meant a trip into space.

There were many men present and eight women, in-eluding Kalna and Ilmuth. The other women were dressed in the same kind of lovely gowns the latter two had worn when first I met them. The men were in comfortable shirts and trousers. Again everyone wore sandals.

Although no introductions were made, I did not miss them, for all greeted me as friends, and a few even called me by name. When the salutations were over, I became aware of soft music in the background, a little reminiscent of what we call Oriental.

Although Ramu had been given a goblet of the juice, I noticed that my other friends did not join us. This was explained when Ilmuth said, "We must go to our posts now to carry out the surprise Kalna mentioned. This time, Ramu will stay with you."

As Orthon and Kalna left in one direction, Firkon and Ilmuth started toward the opposite end of the ship. Ramu and I sipped our drinks in silence for a few moments. I was happy to be a part of the warmth and joyousness that pervaded this room. It helped to keep in the background the feeling of sadness over the parting that would take place tonight.

Several groups were playing games that were strange to me and Ramu, noticing my interest, suggested that we stroll around for a closer view.

Four of the men were seated at a small table playing a game with cards. These were quite different from ours, though much the same size. There were no numbers on them, but all had markings representing something. I looked to see if any two were alike, but, so far as I could see, none were.

Another group of men were rolling little colored balls along a smooth board. I guessed that these must have been charged with some kind of magnetism, since there were no grooves in the board and yet the balls did not move freely. Certain ones seemed to do the attracting, drawing the others toward them.

Another game somewhat resembled our table tennis, except that two balls were kept in play simultaneously, for which great skill was obviously required. The women seemed very good at this.

I was struck by the absence of loud talking, laughing or other distractions. Everyone was obviously enjoying himself, and able to do so without becoming raucous over it as so often happens on Earth. Nor did anyone seem to take the games seriously, as so many of us do. The atmosphere was one of gaiety and relaxation. Often the players glanced up at us with friendly smiles. Some spoke to us and I found myself still amazed to hear these people speaking so fluently in my tongue. After awhile, Ramu suggested, "Shall we go to the control room? There are some things to show you in there which I am certain you will find interesting."

With our drinks still in hand, I gladly followed him into the large room with the many charts, graphs and instruments which I had seen on my first visit to this ship.

As we entered, Ramu must have touched a button for I saw two very small seats rise as if by magic out of the floor. And at the same time, directly in front of them, I saw our Moon appear in the center of a large screen. I was amazed at how close it looked, and not at all as if pictured on a screen, but with depth of space all around it. So this was the surprise! For a moment I thought we might be actually coming in for a landing.

Ramu said, "You are now looking at the familiar side of your Moon, but we are not landing on it. The image is being reflected on the screen from one of the telescopes which was not in operation the first time you were with us. Look closely as we approach the surface and you will note considerable activity. In the numerous large craters which you see from Earth you will notice very large hangars -- which you do not see! Notice, too, that the terrain here is very similar to your deserts.

"We have built these hangars on such a scale in order that much larger ships than this one can enter easily. Also within these hangars are living quarters for a number of workers and their families, provided with every comfort. Water in abundance is piped in from the mountains, just as you have done on your Earth for the purpose of bringing fertility to your desert areas. "When a ship enters these hangars, a process of depressurizing the passengers takes place. This requires about twenty-four hours. Were this not done, the people would experience the greatest discomfort in stepping out on the Moon. Such a depressurization process is not yet conceivable to Earthlings. They understand too little about the bodily functions and their control. Actually, human lungs are able to adjust themselves to very low as well as high pressure, if deflation or inflation is not done too quickly. If hurried, death would result." I would gladly have undergone the necessary deflation for the privilege of actually landing on the Moon. There was nothing demanding my immediate return to Earth.

But with a sympathetic smile, Ramu said, "We have many things in store for you besides showing you the other side of your satellite before we return you to Earth. Watch closely now, for we are approaching the Moon's rim. Notice those clouds forming. They are light and appear to be coming from nowhere, as clouds often do. Most of them gain no density whatsoever but dissipate almost immediately. Yet, under favorable conditions, some occasionally do gain density. It is the shadows of these which have been seen through telescopes from Earth.

"Now we are approaching the side never seen from Earth. Look at the surface directly below us. See, there are mountains in this section. You can even see snow on the peaks of the higher ones, and a growth of heavy timber on the lower slopes. On this side of the Moon are a number of mountain lakes and rivers. You can see one of the lakes below. The rivers empty into a very large body of water.

"Now you can see a number of communities of varying sizes, both in the valleys and on the mountain slopes. Preferences of people here, as anywhere else, vary in regard to living at one or another altitude. And here, as elsewhere, the natural activities to support life are very similar to those wherever mankind is found.

"Had we time to land and be depressurized," Ramu went on, "and then travel about, you would personally meet some of the people. But as far as studying the surface of the Moon is concerned, the way you are viewing it now is far more practical."

I realized the truth of this as a fair-sized city assembled on the screen in front of us. Actually, we seemed to be drifting over the rooftops, and I could see people walking along clean, narrow streets. There was a more thickly built-up central section which I assumed to be the business district, although it was not crowded with people. I noticed no cars of any kind parked along the streets, although I did see several vehicles, moving just *above* the streets, since they appeared to have no wheels. In size they were comparable to our busses, varying from one another in about the same degree.

Ramu explained, "A few of the people here do have their own conveyances, but for the most part they depend on the public utilities at which you are looking."

Just outside the city proper was a comparatively large cleared section with an immense building along one side. It looked like a hangar and Ramu confirmed this by saying, "We have to construct a few hangars near the cities for convenience in landing with the supplies we bring to the population here -- everything not available locally for their needs. In exchange, they furnish us with certain minerals found on the Moon." As I watched, the city seemed suddenly to retreat and Ramu told me that we were now traveling back into space between the Moon and the Earth. "Have you any questions before we return to the lounge?" he asked. I could think of none and shook my head. "In that case," he said, his eyes sparkling, "we had better move on to the lounge. A banquet is in preparation to celebrate the return home of Firkon and myself."

Again I felt ashamed of the emotion that rose at this reminder of the imminent parting, and overcame it by mentally putting myself in their places. Wouldn't I be happy in their circumstance? I would, indeed!

"Any tears I may shed will be for myself alone," I said, striving for the light touch. "For you I am happy."

Orthon and Kalna met us at the door and we entered the lounge together. I saw that the large table on one side of the room had been set for service. Some of the women who had before been playing games were now putting on the finishing touches.

When Firkon and Ilmuth came in by the far door, Kalna joined her friend and the two girls left the room together. In a few minutes they returned, having changed from their pilot suits to lovely flowing robes.

A beautiful cloth of gold and yellow fiber covered the table, woven in colored designs with no definite pattern. Places had been laid the full length and on both sides. The table "silver" was somewhat different in design from ours, and rather improved, I thought. It seemed to be made of various metallic combinations, beautifully inlaid. There was one chair at the head of the table and I counted fourteen on either side. As Kalna and Ilmuth rejoined us, we were asked to be seated. There were still only the eight women present, which left the men twenty-one in number, including myself.

Ramu sat on the master's right and Firkon on his left. Ilmuth was placed between Ramu and myself, and Kalna opposite, between Firkon and Orthon. After all were seated, the master rose and for several moments the room was filled with a reverent stillness. Then, speaking in soft, distinct tones, the great teacher spoke these words:

"We thank the Infinite for present substance. May each and every one within Thy vast kingdom be equally provided. Let this food strengthen our bodies that they may serve the Divine Spirit which dwells within them in ways pleasing to Thee, Creator of all life."

After he had delivered this beautiful prayer, all joined again in a moment of silence.

Then, before resuming his seat, the master said, "We are gathered here tonight to celebrate with great rejoicing the successful fulfillment of the mission on Earth performed by two of our brothers present. Firkon and Ramu have done well. We share their happiness in the reward for their efforts which permits them to return to their home planets.

Crystal clear goblets containing pale golden liquid were on the table before each guest. As the master finished speaking, he raised his glass, saying, "Let us drink in blessing to one another and to our fellow men everywhere."

As I raised the goblet to my lips, I was aware of a most delicate fragrance and sipped the contents very slowly *in* order to lose none of the bouquet. It did not appear to be of an intoxicating nature but perhaps like many wines could have bad that effect if taken in excess.

As we lifted our glasses in honor of Ramu and Firkon, soft music that came from some invisible source filled the room. It was like no music I had ever before heard, seeming to vibrate through all my being; a melody strange and beautiful, with only occasional strains that were similar to Earthly music.

Since this was the first time I had been privileged to dine with those of other worlds, I was naturally curious to learn to what extent their food might resemble ours.

At each end of the table, and in the center, were beautiful bowls filled with fruit. One variety looked exactly like large rosy apples, each with stem intact. I anticipated the crisp juiciness as I accepted one offered to me. Yet when I bit into it, I found the flesh of this fruit had the consistency of a firm, ripe peach, and the flavor was rather like a cross between a cherry and an apple. The core contained one large seed that looked like an immense apple seed.

Another fruit resembled gigantic raspberries, both in appearance and flavor. The smallest of these berries was at least four times the size of our largest.

Placed at intervals along the table were large pitcher-like containers holding a variety of fruit juices and other drinks. This explained the several goblets of different sizes in front of each place. The second drink I tried tasted like pure raspberry juice.

Food was served to us by the two women who bad seated themselves on either side at the end of the long table. First they brought steaming dishes of vegetables from the service table which stood against the wall close by. One contained what looked like ordinary carrots, but I found the consistency not so firm, and the flavor a kind of sweet-sour. A second vegetable looked like the familiar potato. These, though peeled, were served in their natural shape. They had a slight yellow tinge and, although none of the coarse fiber of a parsnip, tasted like that vegetable. Another vegetable which I tried had the leaves and coloring of parsley and a mild lemon flavor.

There were many other vegetables which I did not try. A light eater by nature, tonight my emotions were so divided that I found myself with almost no appetite at all. I tried in vain to banish from my thoughts the purpose of this celebration. Firkon and Ramu, my good friends, would be leaving for their far distant homes....

I did, however, accept a small piece of very coarse and quite dark bread, and a strip of what at first I took to be meat. The bread had a crust of golden color and tasted as though made chiefly of nuts, although I thought I detected a grain flavor as well. As I chewed the brownish strip of "meat" and mentally compared its flavor to that of well-cooked beef, Kalna called to me from across the table.

"That is the dried root of a Venusian plant," she explained. "On Venus we cook the fresh plant, and then it tastes even better, but on our trips we carry it in dried form. It is especially nourishing as it contains all proteins found in meat and is easier for the human body to absorb. One strip of this root as served here is equivalent to one pound of your steak. It also makes excellent seasoning for other foods."

To finish the meal, a huge cake was served. Although this had the appearance of what we call angel food, as it was cut I saw that it did not have the somewhat spongy-elastic consistency of that cake. Moreover, though chiefly white, there were yellow streaks throughout. The texture was very fine and literally seemed to melt in the mouth. It tasted faintly sweet, although when the yellow was separated from the white, the flavor altered in a way difficult to describe. On the whole, I found it delicious.

As I observed the others around the table and listened to their merry conversation, I realized that no one was eating heavily of the abundance of food, as so often happens at banquets on Earth. Yet all seemed to be enjoying it.

At the end of the repast, the women and a number of men arose from their seats and cleared away the dishes. In the miraculous way with which I had become familiar, large doors suddenly opened out into a kitchen from the wall behind the table, which had appeared entirely solid. Into this room everything was carried. In a moment the guests returned to their chairs and the doors closed behind them.

Now the background of music ceased as one of the men rose from his seat. Without accompaniment of any kind, he sang a song in his native tongue. While I could not understand the words, I listened enthralled to the beauty of his voice.

When he had finished, Ilmuth said, "That was a song of farewell and blessing on the Brothers who are returning home." The music rose again from its invisible source, louder than before and with a livelier lilt.

This was explained when two of the women rose and, going to a cleared space beyond the table, began moving to the music in beautiful unison. Later, I was told that the dance represented the power of the Universe.

As I watched, I realized that one would need double joints and the suppleness of an infant to reproduce it. It was truly wonderful to behold, for every motion and posture of their bodies portrayed one after the other, the many moods of nature, from calm waters at rest though the most terrific storms of space.

To describe such rhythm is impossible but it was both fascinating and deeply stirring to behold. The young dancers themselves were exquisitely lovely, and their costumes seemed to change colors while in motion, yet I saw no lights playing upon them. The word "grace" its superlative meaning could not do justice to this beautiful performance.

When the dance was over and a little time had passed, the master spoke to Orthon, who came over to where I was sitting. "Now," he said, "we want to show you scenes from our planet Venus. Scenes that will be beamed directly from the spot to this ship."

I was delighted at the prospect of such a travelogue and wondered on which screen it would appear. But there was no screen. Before my astonished gaze, as the lights dimmed, the first scene hung suspended upon the space of this room!

Orthon seemed to enjoy my amazement and explained, "We have a certain type of projector that can send out and stop beams at any distance desired. The stopping point serves as an invisible screen where the pictures are concentrated with color and dimensional qualities intact."

The scene at which I was looking seemed, in fact, so definitely "there" that it was with the greatest difficulty I could believe myself still on this ship. I saw magnificent mountains, some white-topped with snow; some quite barren and rocky, not very different from those of Earth. Some were thickly timbered and I saw water running in streams and cascades down the mountainsides.

Orthon leaned close to me to whisper, "We have many lakes and seven oceans, all of which are connected by waterways, both natural and artificial."

They showed me several Venusian cities, some large and some small. All gave me the feeling of having been transported to some wonderful fairyland. The structures were beautiful, with no monotonous lines. Many had domes radiating in prismatic colors that gave the impression of a revitalizing force.

"In the dark of the night," Orthon said softly, "the colors cease and the domes become luminous with a soft, yellowish light."

All cities followed a circular or oval pattern, and none appeared in any way congested. Between these concentrated communities there was much still uninhabited territory.

The people I saw on the streets of these cities seemed to be going about their business in much the same manner as Earth folk, except for the absence of rush and worry so noticeable with us. Clothing, too, was similar, each person apparently choosing garments to his own particular liking while following a general style. I would estimate the tallest person I saw to be about six foot six, the average adult about five foot six, and the smallest not over thee foot six. However, this latter could have been a child. I could not be sure, since none show age as we do. I know that I definitely did see some children, much smaller than this particular form. Corresponding to our automobiles for convenience in traveling from one place to another, I saw conveyances patterned somewhat after the mother ship in miniature. They appeared to glide along just above the ground, as had those "busses" I saw on the Moon. These transports varied in size as do our cars, and some had open tops.

I was wondering how they were propelled, which brought Orthon again close to my ear as he explained, "By means of exactly the same energy as operates our space ships."

The streets were well laid out and beautifully bordered with flowers of many colors.

Next, I was shown a beach on the shore of a lake. The sand was very white and fine. Long, low waves rolled in with an almost hypnotic quality. There were many people on the beach and in the water. I wondered what kind of material could be used for their bathing suits as they looked no wetter after a dip in the lake than before.

Kalna, who had come to sit beside me, cleared this up. "The material is not only entirely waterproof but also has properties which repel certain injurious rays from the Sun. Even as on Earth," she went on to explain, "these rays are more powerful when reflected off water than inland."

We were now shown a tropical section of Venus. I was amazed to notice that, in a general sense, many of the trees somewhat resembled our weeping willow since the foliage tended to fall in a kind of cascade effect. The color, however, and details of the leaf were quite different.

As you may imagine, I was very interested in the animal life that entered the various scenes. On the beach I had noticed a small, short-haired dog. Elsewhere, birds of various colors and sizes, little different from ours on Earth. One looked identical to our wild canary. I saw horses and cows in the country, both slightly smaller than those of Earth but otherwise very similar. This seemed to hold true of all animal life on Venus.

The flowers, too, resembled those that grow on our Earth. I would say that the main difference between both animal and plant life on Venus as compared with ours lies in coloring and flesh texture. This, Kalna told me, is due to the ever-present moisture on their planet.

"As you have learned by now," she said, "our people rarely see the stars as you do on Earth. We know the beauties of the heavens beyond our firmament only from our travels and studies."

Last, they showed the picture of a very beautiful woman and her husband with their eighteen children, all but one of whom were fully grown. Yet the parents gave the impression of a young couple in their early thirties.

This ended the showing and I was invited to ask questions. First, I asked what effect, if any, the constant cloudy condition over Venus has on its peoples.

Orthon replied, "In addition to living according to universal laws, our atmosphere is a contributing factor toward an average life span of one thousand years. When the Earth, too, had such an atmosphere, man's years on your planet were correspondingly far greater than now.

"The cloudy formation surrounding our planet acts as a filter system to weaken the destructive rays which otherwise would enter its atmosphere. I call your attention to a record contained within your own Holy Writ. If you study it carefully, you will notice that the span of life on Earth began to decrease when the cloudy formation lessened and men there for the first time saw the stars out in space.

"It may interest you to learn that a gradual tilting of your Earth is even now taking place. If, as could happen at any moment, it should make a complete tilt in order to fulfill its cycle, much of the land now lying under water will rise. For years to come, this water-soaked soil will be in a process of evaporation which will once more cause a constant cloudy formation, or 'firmament' around your Earth. In which case, the life span will again be increased, and if the peoples on your planet learn to live according to the Creator's laws, you too can attain a thousand years in the one body.

"This tilting of your Earth is one reason for the constant observation we are giving it, for its relation to the other planets in our galaxy is very important. A drastic tilt of one planet would, to some degree, affect all, and definitely alter the lanes in which we travel space.

"Surely, any violent tilt would cause a great catastrophe to our Earth, would it not?" I asked.

"That is bound to happen," he replied, "and although the laws which govern the relationship of man to the world on which he lives would not at this present time be understood by men of Earth, I want to stress that the erring path which they have followed so consistently is actually the reason for their ignorance of your planet's present instability. Though the ages, there have been many signs and omens which your people have ignored. Many of these have been recorded in your Holy Writ as prophecies. But your people heeded them not. And although many have already been fulfilled, the lesson has not been learned. It is not wise to become independent of the Creator of all. Mankind must be guided by the hand that has given him life.

"If man is to live without catastrophe, he must look upon his fellow being as himself, the one a reflection of the other. It is not the Creator's wish that mankind turn against itself in cruelty and wanton slaughter."

"I know," I said, "that we are coming into a new cycle of some sort. Some of my brothers on Earth call it the Golden Age, others the Aquarian. Can you throw any light on this?"

"On our planet we do not name the changes in that way, for all we know is progress. But to answer the question for your understanding, we would say that you are approaching the Cosmic Age, however little you may understand this. You have had your Golden Age, worshiping gold more than God. And an Aquarian Age, as you call it, can be only one in which Earth afflicts you with great waters, or not enough. You have passed through both of these conditions. The very naming of the periods of change in this way is a part of the block to your understanding. The Earth people must learn to progress in rhythm with these natural changes and not be subject unto them."

"How," I asked, "would you define the Cosmic Age?"

"Actually, we would rather call it a Cosmic understanding. This is the first time in your civilization that you have, in a broad sense, become aware of the probability of inhabited worlds other than your own. Appearing in our space craft, as we now are doing in such numbers in all the skies of your world, even those who would not believe have little choice. For the first time in the memory of mankind on your planet, there is overwhelming evidence that your planet has not borne life as a kind of freak accident, as even some of your greatest astronomers have stated. Mankind is manifesting on your world because that planet is but one in a vast, orderly creation of the Infinite One, all subject to his Divine laws.

"Our ships perform feats in your skies which no Earthly planes of any nation can do. Your scientists know this. Your governments know this. The pilots of your planes everywhere in your world have seen us and marveled. Thousands of your people have looked up and been amazed. Thousands more everywhere are now watching and hoping for a glimpse of us.

"All this has been foretold by men of old. They have said in your written prophecies that the whole world will be disturbed, and that the signs will be these: Sons of God will be coming from Heaven to Earth to deliver the peoples. The conditions in your world today have placed you, as you put it, under the shadow of death. Your entire world is disturbed. And since the name you have for outer space is 'Heaven,' and since we too are Sons and daughters of God, could it not be that even now the ancient prophecy is being fulfilled?

"It has also been foretold that, when the time cometh, the dark races of the world will rise up and demand the right to equal respect and the lot of free men so long denied them by you of lighter skins. Is not this prophecy, too, being fulfilled in these very days on Earth?

"You see, we know the history of your world well. The conception of 'We are our brother's keeper' applies to all mankind everywhere. It is in this role that we come to you and say, 'Let the Supreme Being of the Universe be the guiding word for your world that your troubles may vanish as darkness before light.' "What would man be without the breath of life? And who giveth unto him? Is it not to be found everywhere for the benefit of all? Then let Earthly man know that his God is not in some far distant place, but ever near in all manifestations, and within Man himself."

Orthon ceased speaking and for a moment I sat with bowed head thinking of his words. Slowly, I became aware of a warmth that seemed to be entering into my spirit. Looking up, I saw from the faces of those around me that what I felt was a benediction that flowed from all of them toward me.

Then the master rose and approached me. As I stood, so did the others.

"My son," he said, looking deeply into my eyes, "much of what our brother has been saying to you is in conflict with many things your people have been taught to believe as truth. This, in itself, is of no importance, since that which was learned yesterday serves only as a stepping stone toward the greater truth we can learn tomorrow. That is the law of progress. Once on the right path, it cannot be otherwise. it is essential always that men work and strive together with open minds, ever aware that all is never known. There is an infallible guide in determining whether the path is a right one. That is very simple. If the results of your thoughts and actions are evil, then the path you are following leads away from the light of His countenance. If good things follow along the way you go, then your lives, and the lives of your children and of their children, will be joyous. Blessings, unbroken by sickness and strife, will be your eternal heritage."

He touched my hand in farewell and left the room in a silence vibrant with the words he had spoken.

I looked long into the faces of my many friends, imprinting each on my memory. There were no spoken f are-wells, but each raised a hand, and I raised mine. Then, i allowed Orthon to lead me along the ways of the carrier back to the little Scout.

Both Firkon and Ramu accompanied me on the drive back to the city. We did not talk.

When we were back at the hotel and the time had come for me to take leave of these dear friends, a feeling of tremendous poignancy engulfed me. We exchanged handclasps and Ramu said softly, "The blessing of the Infinite One go with you.

I left them then, and went on up to my lonely room.

--()--

CHAPTER 15

AN UNEXPECTED POSTSCRIPT

April 25th, 1955

Even as the presses are rolling on the pages of this book, an event of such importance has just occurred that I am recording it here and now to rush to my publishers for inclusion.

All day yesterday, on April the 24th, the usual number of Sunday visitors to my home at Palomar Terraces filled the hours from early until late. As I met and talked with them, I was increasingly aware of being mentally alerted to an approaching visit with the Brothers. It was late when the last couple left and I went to my room and tried unsuccessfully to sleep. Within the hour an urge to get up and go into town became so intense that I knew I must leave without delay.

During the long ride into the city I wondered if a request I had made at our last meeting was going to be answered. I had asked if they would permit me to take photographs *inside* a space ship in order to furnish further evidence to both doubters and believers. Apart from giving me the impression that this might not be so easy of achievement as I seemed to think, one of the Brothers had made a comment which I knew to be true. "Even should we succeed," he pointed out, "I doubt if it would convince the confirmed skeptics for the reason that Earth men still have so false a concept of other planets and the conditions existing thereon."

Nevertheless, I allowed my hope to grow. ...

I went to the usual place and was met by a man to whom I had been introduced at a previous meeting, come to replace a Brother who had returned to his home planet. Without delay we drove to a desert spot where a Scout, identical to the one of my first meeting, waited for us. As we entered the little craft I glanced at my watch and saw that it was exactly 2.30 a.m. After greeting me, the pilot asked if I had brought my camera along. I had indeed! It was a small Polaroid I had recently bought. He had never seen one and asked me to explain the operation.

"This meeting has been arranged specifically to fulfill your hope for the kind of photograph you spoke of when last we met," he said. "We can guarantee nothing for reasons which will be clear to you later, but we shall try to get a picture of our ship with you in it. This would be simple enough if we could use our own method of photography, but that would not serve your purpose. Our cameras and film are entirely magnetic and you have no equipment on Earth that could reproduce such pictures. So we must use yours and see what we can get."

I became so absorbed in explaining the working of the camera to him that I was totally unaware of any movement whatever until the man who had met me called out, "Here we are!"

Looking up, I saw that the Scout's door was opening. Then, to my surprise, I saw that we had landed on top of a small mother ship. "Small" because it was not nearly so large as any I had previously been in. The hatch through which the smaller craft usually entered a carrier was plainly visible but my friend stepped out of the Scout and beckoned me to follow. We walked across the lop of the carrier and past the large hatch to a smaller one which opened as we approached. This was another surprise since I had no idea there were any such openings in these carriers. This turned out to contain an elevator and I was delighted to see Orthon standing on the platform. At his invitation I stepped in beside him. The man who had led me across the carrier returned to the Scout and his companion with whom I had left my camera.

This elevator was similar to the one on the large Saturnian ship, described in Chapter Eight. We lowered to about the middle of the ship where a row of portholes was plainly visible the entire length of both sides of the ship. Here the elevator stopped and we stepped off. Orthon explained that he would stand in front of one porthole and I in front of the one next to it while the men would try to take our pictures from the Scout. The Scout had now moved a little distance away.

I noticed that the portholes of this carrier were double, with about six feet between the outer and the inner glass. We were standing behind the inner windows and I could not help wondering how they could get good pictures with my little camera through all that glass!

It is very difficult to estimate sizes and distances out in space, having nothing with which to compare, but it seemed to me that the Scout was hovering about one hundred feet from the mother ship. From her ball top (see photograph no. 1) she was throwing a beam of bright light upon the larger craft. Sometimes this beam was very intense, and again not so intense. As the photographs show, they were experimenting with the amount of light necessary to show the mother ship and at the same time penetrate though the portholes to catch Orthon and myself behind them.

While this was going on, radiation from both the mother ship and the Scout had been cut to a minimum. I learned later that the men had been obliged to put some sort of filter over the camera and lens in order to protect the film from the magnetic influences of the craft. It was all an initial experiment and, as shown clearly by the photographs, varying distances and intensities of light reflection were tried.

At this point I must admit that I have not ceased to berate myself for my oversight, in the hasty departure for town, in not remembering to bring additional film. This presented a serious handicap to the Brothers by leaving little margin for the trial and error method they were forced to use. As the men worked with my camera, they studied results closely. Perhaps they may be able to make an attachment of one kind or another which will produce more detailed photos at some future date.

It was quite some time before a signal from the Scout indicated that they were returning to the carrier. I watched the elevator as it went up to the top of the ship. The hatch opened and the elevator returned again to our level with the Scout pilot, my camera in his hand. He joined us and reported that although they considered the pictures poor, there had been a measure of success and they had saved the last two exposures to try for photographs of the interior of this carrier.

Having been so well prepared for bad results, I was pleasantly surprised by what he showed me.

As the thee of us walked toward the front of the ship, I saw a wall slide away to reveal an opening very much resembling a tunnel. Beyond this was a small room with two pilots seated at the controls.

Due to the end of the ship being transparent and to the glowing charts inside, there was plenty of light and my hopes ran high for a good picture. All lights in the room where we stood were turned out, leaving it almost entirely dark. But these two attempts failed, due to the greater magnetic power in the carrier in comparison to that in the Scout.

One thing was proven. Without some as yet undeveloped filter system for our film, it is impossible to get clear photographs within the space ships. When I asked if a better camera with a finer lens might be more successful, I was told that any appreciable improvement was unlikely because of the type of film used.

When these last two pictures had been taken, the lights within the ship came on again. The three of us then returned to the elevator and were carried to the top of the ship. As the hatch opened, I saw the Scout again based on its carrier. Orthon touched my hand in farewell and the Scout's pilot and I walked over to the waiting craft. As we entered, the door closed silently behind us and we were immediately on our way.

It is impossible for me to judge how far out in space we had been, but the entire time from leaving the Earth and returning to it was little over two and one half hours.

Back on Earth, my friend and I took leave of the pilot and walked over to where the car was parked. It was shortly before 7 a.m. that my companion let me out at the entrance to my home. Although I invited him to stop for coffee and breakfast, he thanked me and declined, explaining that he must not be late on the job he had taken for the duration of his time here on Earth.

In closing, let me say that I fully realize many attempts will be made to discredit these photographs. This does not disturb me. Every man is free to believe or disbelieve the statements, supported by photographs, that are present in this book. But let each man realize that his personal conclusion in no way alters *the fact of their reality*. For corroboration of this one need only turn the pages of history to almost any year in almost any age. In its mass conception, the Earthbound mind has always found it easier to scoff at new wonders than to face the fact of its own limited knowledge of the miracles that await discovery in the unlimited Universe in which he dwells.

To the Brothers of other worlds, human beings, like ourselves, I am grateful for what they have shown and taught me. To my brothers in this world I report, knowing that many are ready. As always, the skeptics must wait for what, even to them, will be overwhelming proof that space *has* been conquered by peoples from planets far advanced beyond our own.

--()--

GEORGE ADAMSKI

BIOGRAPHICAL SKETCH

Born in Poland April 17, 1891, George Adamski was not yet two years old when his parents emigrated to the United States and settled in Dunkirk, New York. The background of his boyhood was much the same as that of any child of an immigrant family, with one important difference. His parents possessed an unusual and deeply religious approach to the wonders of creation as manifested in the many aspects of nature. Therefore, although the boy's formal school was of short duration, a vital part of his education continued through private instruction. Young George grew into adulthood with wonder and reverence toward all phases of nature.

In such a world, the boy felt, it should be easy for people to live in harmony. Very early he began to search for the reason why they seemed unable to do so. Very early he began to realize that while the ephemeral laws laid down by men were dictated by geography, changing needs and traditions, sometimes by little more than the special interests of those in power, nature's laws were immutable. It seemed to him that the lessons to be found in the pages of history had not been learned. It seemed to him that the peoples of this Earth, individually and collectively, were still walking in old ruts that could lead only to repetition of the same old disasters. It was an absorbing subject to the young Adamski. He knew that, whatever the limitations that surrounded him, to learn all that he could about it would be the enduring quest of his life. With what knowledge he might gain, he hoped to serve his fellow man in some small way.

Fortunately, it did not occur to the boy to harbor any bitterness toward the circumstances which left his parents unable to pay for the kind of education his ambition and keen mind warranted. On the contrary, he voluntarily sought work to help defray the cost of an enlarging family. The university of the world was his, exciting lessons to be learned wherever and with whomever he found himself.

In 1913 Adamski enlisted in the Army, where he served in the 13th Cavalry on the Mexican border, receiving an honorable discharge in 1919. Meanwhile, on Christmas day in 1917 he was married to Mary A. Shimbersky.

Adamski's five years in the Army served but to strengthen his longing to grow in understanding and wisdom that he might be of service to his fellow man. But realizing that the student was not yet equipped to be the teacher, for many years he traveled around the nation, earning his living at any job that offered. It was a good way to study the problems and frustrations from which no man is free. His was no grimly pursued mission, nor was it in his nature to mount a soap box. The blend of patience, compassion and gaiety, so marked in the mature Adamski, must even then have been the qualities which attracted the confidences of his fellow workers.

It was not until he was nearly forty that Adamski called a halt to wandering and settled down at Laguna Beach in California. This was his first real home and here, through the nineteen thirties, he devoted full time to teaching the universal laws. His students soon numbered into the hundreds, he found himself in demand for lectures throughout Southern California and his talks were broadcast over radio stations KFOX in Long Beach and KMPC in Los Angeles.

One of his students presented him with a six-inch Newtonian reflecting telescope and Adamski spent much time studying the heavens. He and his students took innumerable photographs with homemade attachments. It was during this period that Adamski got his first photograph of a space craft, although at the time he did not know what it was. The photograph was submitted to several astronomers. None could identify it. The object was too far out in space for details to show up. A number of guesses were made which no one considered satisfactory.

In 1940, foreseeing war in the offing, Adamski and a few of his students whose circumstances permitted moved from Laguna Beach to a settlement along the route to Palomar Mountain called Valley Center. Here they labored diligently on establishing a small farming project which they hoped would make them self-sustaining for the duration. When America entered the war, Adamski served his locality as an air-raid warden.

In 1944 the Valley Center Ranch was sold. Adamski and the small group who had remained with him during the war years moved to the southern slopes of Mt. Palomar, six miles below the crest of that mountain and eleven miles from the site of the world's largest telescope, at that time uncompleted. Here they cleared virgin land and built simple living quarters. Here also they raised a small building to serve as a café for passers-by, owned and operated by Mrs. Alice K. Wells, one of Adamski's students. Each member of the group shared in the manual labor that went into this effort, and since heavy restrictions were still in effect regarding materials, anything available had to serve.

Adamski bought a 15-inch telescope and a small observatory was erected to house this, designed in a way which enabled *him* to study the skies for hours on end, protected from inclement weather. The smaller 6-inch telescope was mounted out in the open. In this way, Adamski was able to continue his studies of the skies. Many visitors were interested and with these he gladly discussed his findings.

During the meteoric shower of 1946 Adamski and a number of friends watching with him witnessed a dramatic event, unrecognized for what it was at the time. They observed a large cigar-shaped craft hanging motionless in the skies at comparatively close range. A completely strange object to all, none guessed its true origin. Although Adamski had long discussed the probability of human life on other planets, he still held the opinion that distances between even our closest heavenly neighbors were far too great for any physical interplanetary travel. Only in the following year (1947) came proof that he was mistaken. With his wife and a few associates, for more than an hour Adamski watched a formation of unearthly craft moving without sound in orderly single file across the heavens from East to West.

Since this same display had been witnessed by other groups in different localities, during the following weeks many persons came to Adamski to check their personal observations. Not one could believe that the awesome spectacle could be accounted for by any craft as yet made on our Earth.

Adamski's further experiences in this field have been given to the public in the book *Flying Saucers Have Landed*, co-authored with Desmond Leslie. Events which have occurred since that publication have been recounted in this present book.

Charlotte Blodget

End

--()--

Made in the USA
Las Vegas, NV
12 May 2023

71943342R00059